# Peak Performance Selling

## Also by Kerry Johnson

*New Mindset, New Results*

*Why Smart People Make Dumb Mistakes With Their Money*

*Willpower*

*Mastering Self-Confidence with NLP*

*Phone Sales*

*Sales Magic*

*Trust-Based Selling*

*How to Read Your Client's Mind*

# Peak Performance Selling

## How to Increase Your Sales by 80% in 8 Weeks

Kerry Johnson, MBA, Ph.D.

Published 2019 by Gildan Media LLC
aka G&D Media
www.GandDmedia.com



FIRST EDITION 2019

Front cover design by David Rheinhardt of Pyrographx

Interior design by Meghan Day Healey of Story Horse, LLC

Library of Congress Cataloging-in-Publication Data is available upon request

ISBN: 978-1-7225-0178-5

10 9 8 7 6 5 4 3 2 1

# Contents

# Preface

Many people claim that the keys to success are goal setting and goal planning. But that is only the beginning. Success comes from goal *getting*. To achieve the results you want, you must first understand the psychology of producing those results.

Why do people succeed or fail?

Why do New Year's resolutions rarely make it to year-end?

What are the stressful effects of change?

Why do many people fear doing things that yield high rewards?

This book discusses why we need goals and what goals can do for us. It will provide you with a blueprint for attaining goals. It will help you analyze how much effort you will need to achieve your goals. It will also show you how to cope with the stress that might result from increasing your sales performance quickly.

## The Peak Performance Program

This book will provide all the information you'll need to increase your business dramatically. The basis of this program, which is founded on a psychology of performance, is clearly outlined in chapters 1 through 9. The specifics of the program—complete with charts and guidelines—are included in chapters 10 through 17.

Changing old habits or establishing appropriate new habits will be an integral part of your performance program. Research has shown that correct habits are the gateway to achievement. Forming and modifying habits are critical factors in goal getting (see chapter 13).

Part of the program is to become involved in a performance partnership (see chapter 17), since it is much easier to achieve goals when you have to be accountable to someone else and when you have someone to share your successes with.

The elements of this program are designed so you can produce a personalized program that can help you achieve your goals. Applying the program—which you will adapt for your needs, using your personal goals and behavior as a foundation—you can work over the next six to eight weeks to get what you want.

## Applications

You can apply your performance program to virtually any situation in your life for which a goal can be set. Results are guaranteed if you follow your program faithfully.

The successful applications are widespread. People have taken off weight and maintained the self-discipline to stay on their diets. Parents have radically improved their children's behaviors. Managers in all types of businesses have drastically improved their own and their employees' performance. Using this program over the past several years, my staff has witnessed some incredible results. All of those who completed it have increased their performance and profitability at least 80 percent over an eight-week period—and some as much as 400 percent over the same period! But more importantly, these people have kept their high levels of performance over many months and years.

## How This Book Can Increase Your Business

All of us can achieve much more than we do. In fact, right now you could probably name several things you would like to do differently in both your personal and business life. Some of these modifications could very well mean the difference between $125,000 per year and $550,000 per year.

This program will help you develop a system to assist you in achieving greater productivity and better performance in your current job. The bottom line is you can achieve greater satisfaction and make more money. This program can help you make quantum leaps in your productivity and, as a result, in your income.

First, we will examine what prevents you from achieving maximum performance. There are important psychological barriers to hitting your goals—certain behaviors that make you a slave to your own insecurities. Understanding what these behaviors are and what they do will help you overcome these obstacles.

Second, we will examine the four greatest fears: fear of success, fear of failure, fear of embarrassment, and fear of rejection. We also look at how these fears may be sabotaging your success and your ability to achieve. We will examine the success characteristics of some of the world's richest, most famous, and most successful people. From them we can learn a lot about setting and planning objectives, as well as how to make these objectives work for us.

Finally, we focus on habits, habit patterns, and how they affect us. We help you understand how habits are formed, why many habits are so difficult to break, and how to modify or change present habits or form new ones. Doing this will help you *achieve* what you *conceive* and *believe* you want. You will be introduced to the psychological concept of conditioning and study its relationship to achievement. You will also learn how it can be used to change or modify your habits.

## Coping with Change

Change is one of the most difficult processes we face. Nevertheless, change is a constant, dynamic part of life; it occurs regularly. And it can bring on stress. You will learn how about how stress helps you on the one hand and, on the other, how to manage stress as a part of the performance process. To become and remain productive, you will need to learn to cope with stress. This book will introduce you to many stress-management techniques. We also cover ways to keep you from burning out while your performance is skyrocketing and you are increasing your profitability.

Finally, we combine all these factors into a program to achieve your goals.

## The Facts versus Psychological Performance Skills

In this book, we will concentrate on behavioral or psychological performance skills. Companies often help us in two areas: technical and administrative skills. They improve technical skills by educating you about their product, sending you to school to learn how to use their processes, or otherwise assisting you in carrying out your job more effectively.

Many companies spend thousands teaching employees about a job's technical aspects so they will perform successfully. For example, if you sell life insurance, your company will teach you all about products like whole- or term-life insurance policies. If you are a bedframe salesperson, you will learn about 10D bedsprings. When a new product emerges, such as universal life insurance or 10F bedsprings, the company is quick to provide all necessary data and training to enable you to successfully market the product. In financial services, they may also even teach you about taxation, financial planning, and accounting.

Companies are always willing to tell you the hard facts about their products and services. But they rarely teach how to manage yourself or how to work with other people. Management and sales skills usually aren't covered.

A recent study conducted by Harvard University showed that a great majority of people who retire, resign, or are fired from a business don't leave because they can't handle the work or are incompetent. They depart because of their inability to get along with others—they are ultimately unable to cope with the frustration and discouragement they face in their everyday work lives.

Basically, companies tell us what to do and even teach us how to do it. But rarely will they ever tell us how to motivate ourselves or get along with others.

## The Frustrated Manager

Most companies train minimally in sales and management. For example, a well-trained salesperson has some basic communication techniques, both verbal and written. Some may know how important it is to listen before trying to persuade. Some managers may have even been exposed to participative leadership or gaining consensus before making an important decision. But few managers are trained in motivating employees. They are rarely taught about the real frustrations and problems in dealing with people.

## The Human Factor—Psychological Performance

Behavioral or psychological productivity skills are also often ignored by companies when training employees. In this book, we will concentrate on these skills. They can help you change your life and increase your productivity.

# PART ONE

# WHY YOU'RE HOLDING BACK

# One

# Overcoming Limitations to Performance

In the last six weeks have you procrastinated?

Not prospected enough?

Not asked for enough referrals?

Found that when you finally got around to organizing your messy desk, it was during prime business or selling time?

## Avoidance Behaviors—Symptoms of a Problem

If you said "yes" to any of these questions, you are practicing avoidance behaviors. Avoidance behaviors are the things we do to keep from feeling psychological discomfort. If left to run rampant, they can destroy productivity.

As a consultant, I constantly deal with folks who exhibit obvious avoidance behaviors. Some people in the businesses I work with are incredibly unproductive.

The issue is probably not that they don't know what to do. These managers or employees have typically spent many years learning their jobs. Their knowledge and experience are quite sufficient.

Why don't these people do what they know they should do to double or even triple their level of productivity? Could they be lazy—or it is simply that they want to avoid the discomfort that the change to a higher productive state may bring?

I recently hired a staff person to do follow-up marketing calls. A basic part of her job was to call people who were interested in using our services. Unfortunately, she consistently found ways to avoid making those calls. Her avoidance behaviors included typing out forms to keep track of the phone calls, or reorganizing the filing system to make the resource materials more accessible. All of them were to avoid making the calls that stressed her out so much.

While it was obvious that making calls was the most important thing to do at the time, she risked her job by not doing it. Was this laziness, or was it an unconscious desire to avoid the discomfort those phone calls brought?

Time-management programs promise higher productivity. Unfortunately, many people who spend upwards of $180 to $250 for a day-long seminar often don't seem able to change their behavior enough to reach the promised level of performance.

Why don't people use their time more effectively after they come back from a time-management seminar? Why don't they make more calls, answer more letters, and get rid of useless pieces of paper on their desk?

The answer may lie in avoidance behaviors. To immediately erase all avoidance behaviors from your life and instead practice the desired time-management techniques, you would need to change a great deal all at once. Very few people become that efficient that quickly on their own, often because of underlying subconscious reasons that cause them to be disorganized in the first place. These reasons manifest themselves in avoidance behaviors.

We've all seen avoidance behaviors at work, both in ourselves and in coworkers. These behaviors may include shuffling cards around the desk, arriving at work late, leaving early, taking an extralong lunch, or even reading a book or magazine on the job.

Pause for a minute. Can you think of avoidance behaviors you engage in in your own life? Do you spend thirty or forty minutes chatting with associates or friends in your office before you get down to the business of making phone calls or dealing with difficult projects? Do you read your mail during the 8-to-5 workday, knowing that it may be the least productive use of your time?

As you might have guessed, avoidance behaviors are not the actual problem. They are merely the symptoms. They indicate that you may be experiencing a psychological dilemma on a much deeper level, or a variety of self-sabotaging fears.

## Self-Sabotaging Fears

I like to joke that human beings are only born with three great fears—(1) fear of falling; (2) fear of loud noises; (3) fear of the IRS—and that all other fears are learned responses.

More seriously, the four self-sabotaging fears are simply learned responses. But if they go unchecked, these fears are nothing to kid about and can seriously impair your performance. These four fears are:

- Fear of rejection
- Fear of embarrassment
- Fear of failure
- Fear of success

Each of these fears is discussed at length in chapters 3 through 6. Erasing them is one of the first steps to increasing your productivity. Techniques for doing so are found in chapters 8 and 9.

## Performance Barriers

We all face psychological barriers to goal achievement, often daily in our business and personal lives. These performance barriers are not likely to go away by themselves, because they are frequently symptoms of much larger and deeper issues. But in order to rid ourselves of these barriers, we must first become aware of their existence.

But first let's examine some symptomatic behaviors that limit our productivity. They include:

- Procrastination
- Disorganization
- Lack of motivation

The first problem behavior is *procrastination*: putting things off intentionally and habitually. When we procrastinate, we do not accomplish tasks when we know they should be done but postpone them until the very last moment.

The word *procrastinate* is derived from the Latin *pro*, meaning *toward*, and *cras*, meaning *tomorrow*. I'm sure you've heard the saying, "Don't put off until tomorrow what you should do today."

Usually we procrastinate because we are faced with a difficult task we don't want to do. The task might require anxiety-provoking emotional involvement, like paying bills. Or we may be afraid of making mistakes, for example when talking to intimidating people. So we simply put these things off. Procrastination not only limits performance, but also can counter productivity.

When you procrastinate, you might often find yourself asking yourself:

"What did I do today?"

"Why didn't I accomplish what I wanted to accomplish?"

"Why didn't I achieve what I had planned?"

You feel guilty because you didn't meet your own expectations. Your self-confidence is threatened. In turn, your performance decreases. Think of the last sixty days. How many times have you ended up losing a sale or ruining a big deal because you procrastinated—you waited until the last moment, put something off, or didn't do it at all?

The second performance barrier is *disorganization*. Do you find it difficult to locate things in your office? Do you fail to keep track of your ideas? Of things you've talked about? Are you spending too much time looking up information that should be at your fingertips? If you were more organized, would you cease to neglect doing those things you know would make you more efficient and productive?

Disorganization as a barrier to productivity is certainly not a new concern. Entire seminars are devoted to time management. Numerous books go into great detail about becoming organized and include ways to think about time and your physical environment.

Surprising as it might seem, remember that, by nature, people recognize and like to replicate patterns. Human beings *like* to be organized. There is nothing in your horoscope that predestines you to plague yourself with disorganization.

The causes of disorganization are primarily psychological, stemming from childhood as well as from the challenge of coping with a highly complex world. Many disorganized people are in essence still challenging childhood authority, usually that of a parent.

Parents teach their young children that there are ways things "ought" to be, that there is a "right" way to do things, and that a "good" child is "disciplined" and "orderly." The demands parents make and the attitudes they instill in their children toward life affect them deeply.

Most parents have begged their children in this way: "Jeff, clean up your room." Depending on the circumstances, the child may interpret this demand as an infringement on his identity and autonomy. At some point defiance begins. The child begins to resent the parental control and tends to rebel, in effect saying to the parents, "I won't be orderly or disciplined." So he or she fights the parents' authority in the belief that order means entrapment or loss of identity and that disorder means freedom from parents and greater self-identity.

My experiences with my daughter Catherine are a prime example of how disorder and rebellion towards parents can manifest. Even though my wife, Merita, asked her daily to pick up things lying in her room, she usually made a point of throwing pajamas on the floor, spreading her toys across the bed, and causing her room to look as though a bomb had struck.

At first glance, it seems to be a natural childhood function to be disorderly. When we dig deeper, however, we find that the disorganization often comes from a child's refusal to do everything the authority figures have demanded. This is because the child needs to establish an identity. In fact, when Merita asked our daughter Caroline to eat a little more slowly, she would sometimes slams her fork down and exclaim, "I don't want to eat anything at all!" To many children, a very simple request becomes an intolerable order.

The problem also manifests itself later in life. When executives' desks are so disorganized that they can barely find things, and their secretaries are constantly after them to clean up the desk, or asking,

"Where is the Smith account or the Kellermark research?" Executives know they should be organized, but for some reason, they continue to be disorganized, even though it may be destroying their business.

Does the executive simply have bad business skills, or is he or she rebelling against authority? Perhaps the executive rebels because on some level the secretary's authority in running the office reminds him or her of a parent scolding about picking things up in a room.

The most characteristic way people cope with the emotional conflict of order versus disorder is by developing an attitude of compliant defiance.

Most people desperately want to be correct. They yearn to have their lives organized the way they "ought to be." This is compliance—the conscious acceptance of parental standards. These people set exaggerated goals and, because these goals are unrealistic and often irrelevant to anything practical, the person adopts the attitude of compliant defiance and says, "The heck with it. I can't do it and I won't." This attitude precipitates feelings of failure, because we begin to see ourselves as unable to live up to the parents' or parental authority's expectations, which we have consciously accepted.

## The Need for Order

The elements of real order include a physical environment that is easy to move around in, look at, and function in. Order is a simple necessity for dealing effectively with the volume of paperwork and money matters which we all must confront. Order is whatever helps us to function effectively. We define our particular purposes and create an order—the practical systems that allow us to function effectively and live purposeful lives.

Everyone is capable of being organized. We have a powerful inner drive toward order and clarity. Being disorganized is an avoidance behavior symptomatic of anxiety resulting from the four self-sabotaging fears we will discuss in chapters 3 through 6.

A third business performance barrier is *lack of motivation*. If you answer "yes" to any of the following questions, chances are you are experiencing a lack of motivation:

Do you sometimes feel that all you want to do is sit there?

Do you not want to dial the telephone, talk to prospects, or talk to people at all?

Do you find that your self-esteem is diminishing a bit or that you have no real enthusiasm or excitement for the work you're doing right now?

Do you feel some sense of worthlessness because you're not meeting your self-expectations?

In your job, are you avoiding some activities that cause you discomfort?

Sometimes a lack of motivation results from a feeling of complacency. Because of the anxiety the process of change brings, we merely resist change itself.

Beware of "rah-rah" motivational speakers who capitalize on our emotional vulnerability. Most motivational speakers who claim they can help deliver us from our lack of passion rarely fulfill their claims. Many attendees of motivational programs feel great immediately afterward, but rarely can remember what the speaker said.

Recently I was a keynote speaker at a large real-estate industry convention. After my presentation, I got the chance to talk with the program chairperson at length about some of the speakers she contracted earlier in the year. One of them, a motivational, positive-mental-attitude type, spoke at their conference in Texas.

The attendees remembered him as a marvelous and gifted speaker with enormous rapport and enthusiasm. Unfortunately, no one could remember anything he said, nor had people left with any techniques, skills, or ideas they could use to improve their business or personal lives.

The late Jim Rohn, author of the book, *The Seven Keys to Wealth and Happiness*, saw the same attendees over and over at his speeches. Jim used to tell them, "I've seen a lot of you before. How come you're in another motivational seminar? Didn't you apply the techniques you learned last time?"

Jim's point is basically that you can't get motivation from a speaker or by reading a motivational book. If you ever played Little League baseball or school sports, you likely had a coach who gave a motivational pep talk before a game. That pep talk lasted for about twenty, maybe even thirty minutes. But the performance you gave was the result of your internal motivation, not the coach's pleas. You remember the coach said, "Do your best," but you probably had a tough time remembering anything else.

Many motivational speakers are entertaining and enjoyable. But until you are able to set a plan for yourself to achieve your objectives, you might as well be throwing money into a rathole.

Motivation comes from within. Motivation does not come from being pumped up externally. Motivation is an internal process. Another person can set the stage, but only you can act out the part and motivate yourself. You are the only one who can change yourself. No one can do it for you. This book is dedicated to helping you make the changes you desire.

# Two

# Self-Sabotaging Fears

## How Learned Behaviors Cause Production to Plummet

While many outside factors affect our productivity, there are some things we do to ourselves that limit our own performance. They are called self-defeating or self-sabotaging behaviors, otherwise known as irrational fears. As I've already noted, these fears are:

- Fear of rejection
- Fear of embarrassment
- Fear of failure
- Fear of success

To some extent, all of us probably have these fears. They do more to stifle our success than lifelong economic depression. These fears are not realistic or rational. A rational fear, for example, would be if you were afraid that your car, a '56 Chevy which has conked out twice this week, is going to break down on the highway soon. That fear would certainly be realistic. Or if you haven't made payments for the last six months, a fear that the bank might foreclose on your house would be rational and realistic. Self-sabotaging fears are unrealistic and irrational. We have all at some time been infected with them.

## Anxiety and Depression

Common symptoms of self-sabotaging fears are anxiety and depression. While anxiety may not be a constant or overwhelming problem for you, it may arise at the worst possible time, perhaps when you are making cold calls or trying to persuade someone to buy a product or service or even to accept your ideas.

Let's say you go into a prospect's or client's office. You've known this person for years and expect him or her only to say something like, "After hearing that presentation, I'll give you two orders." But then he quickly gives you a real zinger: "Get out and stay out!" Would you feel rejected? Chances are you would. But there is no real reason to fear somebody who is not receptive to all of your ideas. That goes with the territory. Such a fear is irrational.

A rational fear in the same situation might come if that same client said, "Get out and stay out," then reached for an axe above the fireplace. Your feeling not only of rejection, but also of fear, would be highly rational. The truly rational person would have the good sense to flee the premises.

Let me give you another example of the difference between irrational and rational fears. I have a very irrational fear of driving in bumper-to-bumper Los Angeles freeway traffic. It usually makes my heart pound faster and gives me headaches and hot flashes.

But many years ago, I had a very rational fear when a friend of mine took me into Los Angeles rush-hour freeway traffic in his 1972 Ford Pinto. I called it the "Hindenburg on wheels." It even had flammable Firestone 500 tires. When I told him how nervous I was about the Pinto's reputation for rear-end gas-tank explosions, he said, "Kerry, don't worry. Ford recalled all its Pintos. They installed smoke detectors in the trunks."

## Creating the Fears

One basic premise of this book is that the fears now sabotaging your business and your personal life are largely self-created. They exist within us, generally as a result of the way we were brought up. The big culprits many years ago were our parents, siblings, and friends.

These fears cause anxiety and depression and produce behaviors that are productivity barriers, discussed in chapter 1—such as procrastination, disorganization, or lack of motivation. Other behaviors that might result from self-sabotaging fears are displays of anger or frustration.

Chapters 3 through 6 familiarize you with the self-sabotaging fears, how they affect your performance, and how you can get rid of them to increase your productivity.

# Three

# Self-Sabotaging Fear Number One: Fear of Rejection

Almost 50 percent of business failures have been linked to fear of rejection. What's more, fear of rejection has a direct impact on how profitable businesspeople can be.

Few of us can cope with being rejected on a constant basis. Most of us feel a need to be accepted by others. Many can't even stand occasional rejection.

Salespeople may display fear of rejection by being reluctant to ask prospects if they would like to buy a product or place an order. This is because many salespeople feel they have a friendship or personal relationship when selling a product to a prospect. When asked to buy, the prospect may say no, causing the salesperson deep anxiety.

When a salesperson hesitates to ask the prospect to buy, this is clearly a case of fear of rejection. The fear of rejection mainly occurs when we don't want to hear the word *no*.

We all experience it. In 1976, I was blessed with the opportunity to play on the European Grand Prix Tennis Tour. I had a few financial backers, but I really needed the support of one of the tennis-racket companies, especially since they could supply my equipment.

I set up a meeting with a major sporting-goods company. I went into the office of the marketing vice president and declared: "You don't want to sponsor me on the Grand Prix Tour, do you?" Clearly my presentation was an unconscious effort on my part to get him and myself to expect a no. I didn't want to get my hopes up expecting a yes only to be surprised by a no.

Think about it. Given my approach, wouldn't it have been difficult for the executive to say yes when I so thoroughly prompted him into saying no?

I had sabotaged myself because of my fear of rejection, even though I desperately tried to avoid rejection with this company. I ultimately did approach another major company. But this time, instead of giving the executive and myself a predetermined decision of no, I sold myself well. I walked into this vice president's office and simply said, "My name is Kerry Johnson. I play professional tennis, and I would like to help you sell more tennis rackets."

When he asked me if I had any selling experience, I said, "No, but that is not what I meant." I told him simply and clearly that I would give him something much more valuable than time selling his tennis rackets store to store. I told him that I could sell his rackets to hundreds of thousands of people in the same time it would usually take one of his salespeople to sell one. I explained that I would prominently display his company's rackets any time I played in a tournament. I explained that I would take care to display his company's equipment if there was to be television coverage of the match.

Seeing a good opportunity for promotion and disregarding my exaggeration, he promptly gave me nine complimentary rackets and told me to display them whenever I could.

After my first failed attempt with the other company, I had become much clearer about what I wanted. I realized I had little to lose in taking a bolder approach. I decided to hit my fear of rejection head-on.

Needless to say, I was nervous and anxious, and would rather have sucked on a lemon for two straight days than ask this executive to do something I feared he'd say no to. Nonetheless, I found that, even after my initial failure, the door of opportunity has a higher potential for opening when you knock twice.

When I conquered my fear of rejection with the second potential sponsor, I was no stranger to that fear. In my teenage years, the fear of rejection had already begun to manifest itself. I remember one beautiful sweetheart of a girl named DruAnn. I knew I was in love with DruAnn. The problem was I doubted she even knew I existed.

We had fifth-period class together and sat side by side. During the break after class, I maneuvered myself next to her and started a conversation. But as we walked, for some reason I couldn't bring myself to ask her for a date—I was too nervous, too anxious. I would have been completely crushed if she had rejected me by saying no.

I tried to get up some nerve, but I hesitated, avoided eye contact with her, and stuttered as I tried to make conversation. Finally, I gave up and left, since she gave me no great help.

My fear of being rejected by DruAnn was so intense that it caused me to behave in an overly shy, submissive manner. My irrational fear of rejection sabotaged my chances of getting a date.

Fear of rejection also plagues salespeople who don't ask for referrals because they simply don't want the prospect or client to say no. They experience anxiety and frustration just thinking about asking someone for a referral.

## Primary and Secondary Fears

Probably every businessperson has experienced fear of rejection at one time or another. There are actually two levels of this fear: *primary fear of rejection* and *secondary fear of rejection*. Examples of primary fears include:

- Acrophobia, the fear of heights.
- Hydrophobia, the fear of water.
- Agoraphobia, the fear of being in open places. People with this fear are often even afraid to go outside their homes for fear that something bad will happen to them.

A recent study by the psychology department at New York University found that approximately 35 percent of the U.S. population suffers from some sort of mental illness. Neurotic manifestations of mental illness tend to be anxiety and depression, which are also symptoms of primary fears.

Salespeople with a primary fear would probably never be in a selling-related business, nor would they put themselves in a position of trying to persuade other people to be their clients, do business with them, or contribute money for a fundraiser or other project.

About a year ago in Washington, D.C., I spoke to a large convention of insurance agents. One agent, in his late twenties, walked up after my program and asked if it was true that some people just didn't have the right stuff to be top sales professionals. I told him that was probably true, but it's more a case of having a primary fear than of not having the right talents and attributes.

A secondary fear of rejection is different. With secondary fears, we might enjoy talking to people, but we would avoid selling to them. We might try to get them to buy our product or ask for a contribution for the new music center only by explaining and *not* trying to persuade.

To understand how someone might display a secondary fear of rejection, let's take the example of a mailman who is pulled into a job as a telephone solicitor. Perhaps the mailman chose to work for the Postal Service and enjoyed doing so because he wouldn't have to experience rejection. He provides a needed service: he sorts and organizes mail, and when he deals with the public, he does not have to persuade them to buy stamps or to ask for postal rates.

But say we put that same mailman on the telephone to set up appointments with people he has never met. He probably would have an anxiety attack.

A secondary fear of rejection can keep us from increasing our productivity and performance, and it can limit our profitability on the job. But that does not mean we are in the wrong career. It only indicates we have some anxieties about dealing with people we must try to persuade.

A few years ago, some of my researchers did a study on 423 sales and marketing professionals. The study was done to uncover affects and symptoms of primary and secondary fears. More than 95 percent of the professionals surveyed said they experienced fear of rejection at least once a week. We jokingly concluded the other 5 percent lied.

## Factors in Fear of Rejection

Our overall fear of rejection is affected by the repetition, severity, and duration of the rejections. These factors determine how much rejection we can handle before we start to use avoidance behaviors to avoid it altogether.

## REPETITION

The repetition factor is determined by how often you're rejected. For example, you may be able to tolerate ten rejections in one day, but not fifteen. Or perhaps you can handle eight, but not ten. If you get any more rejections than you can handle, you start exhibiting avoidance behaviors like daydreaming, pushing papers around your desk, calling up friends, and spending increasing amounts of time talking to people. You may even leave the office at noon and play golf or tennis for the rest of the day. Each of these behaviors is an effort to avoid more rejection.

In my business, the repetition factor involves dealing with about six negative or difficult people on the telephone. When I encounter this level of resistance, I typically start using avoidance behaviors, such as writing letters by hand instead of dictating them with a voice-recognition system. I overread my email. I've even read through my spam, which is obviously a waste of time. My favorite avoidance behavior is taking fifteen- to twenty-minute breaks. I'll chat with my secretary or other salespeople down the hall to take away the anxiety my recent rejection gave me.

## SEVERITY

When we fear rejection by certain people who may be especially intimidating or whom we perceive as so important that a rejection from them makes us feel devastated, we are experiencing the severity factor of the fear of rejection. On a one-to-ten scale, rejection by such people would register an eight or nine.

The severity factor is also triggered if someone is verbally abusive to us while we're selling. You know the type: the prospect who says, "Don't ever call me again."

Here are a few questions you can ask yourself to uncover whether you are suffering from severity-factor rejection fears:

Do you sincerely believe that you are selling in a market or at a level below your ability?

Do you feel that you might be working below your potential?

Do you avoid certain people?

If your answer is yes to any of these questions, you may be experiencing a severity factor.

We can understand how this factor works if we contrast two situations. In the first, let's say you're a salesperson who happens to be at home when the letter carrier knocks at your door. You might attempt to get into a conversation with the letter carrier and even start giving a sales pitch. The letter carrier then might say, "Leave me alone, I'm busy." You would probably think, "Who cares? It's not a high-revenue sale anyway."

In the second situation, a professional, or someone you deeply respect, says no to a sales pitch. Then you feel the pain of rejection. Because of the severity factor, you feel psychological discomfort at a higher level than you did with the letter carrier.

Most of us do our best to avoid receiving rejection from people we greatly respect. When these people say no or reject us, we typically feel much more severe anxiety than with others.

## DURATION

The duration factor involves how often we are rejected by the same person or in the same situation. If we are constantly rejected by someone we contact once a month, the duration factor may begin to cause us to use avoidance behaviors to stay clear of those scenes, which have a high potential for rejection.

Maybe we've had a boss who has nothing nice to say about our production or performance level. In fact, every time the boss gives us a performance appraisal, he or she only gives us negative feedback. Chances are we will begin to experience the duration factor taking hold in our fear of rejection.

Experts in the financial-planning industry, as well as in real estate and other sophisticated businesses, know that it often takes more than one contact with someone to get some business. Often it takes five or six contacts just to get in the door. The problem is that if we experience the duration factor, it will be difficult to get past the first no, negative person, or tough situation. We then would become doomed to spending much of our business life repeatedly failing to find ways to get past the initial rejection stage, rather than being persistent and showing ingenuity in overcoming the repeated rejections and getting the business.

I recently sat next to a delightfully attractive sixty-year-old woman on an airline flight. Her husband was asleep in the window seat next to her. After I had spent a half hour talking to her, he suddenly woke up and screamed, "Mildred, shut up!" and then went back to sleep.

I whispered to the woman, "How long have you been married?"

"Twenty-three years," she said. "Twenty-three miserable years."

"How come you are still married to this guy?"

She responded, "I know he will change any day now."

The duration factor in fear of rejection clearly had a strong hold on her.

All of the factors above can be overcome. But before attempting to deal with them, you need to know how you let them start to affect you. How did you get this malady called the fear of rejection, and the factors that go along with it?

## Socialization Leads to Fear of Rejection

Most of us were socialized by our parents and peers to have some fear of rejection. Mom and Dad would say, "Don't talk to any strangers," or, "Don't talk to people you don't know," or "You should stay away from shifty-looking people." The problem is when you're young, everybody look shifty and most people are strangers.

Our peers socialize us to be perpetually worried about what people think of us. Remember asking your best friend when you were a teenager, "Do you think she likes me?"

We are so desperate for people to like us that we avoid disagreements for fear of what they'll think of us. This socialization instills a deep need to be accepted and an avoidance of rejection at all costs.

But if salespeople never got rejection, commissions would be cut in half. Without a fear of rejection and the skill to overcome it, selling would be so easy that anyone could do it.

If you can get over your need to be accepted by others—your fear of rejection—your sales and business will dramatically improve.

Society has inappropriately conditioned us to place too much importance on whether someone likes us or not, and not enough importance on liking ourselves. The most successful business pros and persuaders put a lot more weight on how they feel about themselves than on how other people feel about them.

When I first started my business-psychology practice, I received more rejection than most people experience during their entire careers. I realized that one of the best marketing tactics for my sales and management training expertise was to go to existing insurance agencies and work for practically nothing to gain experience.

I had gotten hold of a directory called *Contacts Influential*, which included the names of many people at these agencies. One way I promoted myself was simply to make cold calls on the people in the directory. I made as many calls as I could. An experienced sales executive friend taught me to ask for a face-to-face appointment by saying, "I'd like to see you Tuesday at 3 p.m. or Wednesday at 4 p.m. Which is best for you?"

In most cases, this close was ineffective. The company owner or manager would simply reply, "Yes, I know phone sales techniques too. You're going to have to tell me more about why you want to see me."

When one by one, each of these prospects said no to me, I constantly promised myself I would get an 8-to-5 job with a company to avoid the psychological pain I was experiencing. I sincerely believed at the time that they were really saying, "I don't like you. I don't want to talk to you. Leave me alone."

The rejection caused anxiety because of my overabundant need for others to like and respect me. Even years after that initially horrendous rejection experience, I still had difficulty accepting objections effectively. But as you are probably aware, when an individual gives you an objection, they are really saying, "You have not yet persuaded me yet that I can benefit by meeting with you."

If you were to picture a scale with a balance point on either side, these objectors would be seeing one side of the scale as being substantially higher than the other.

In my case, when someone gave me an objection such as "We really can't use you for our convention; we don't have enough time for a presentation as complex as yours," I felt rejected. In cases like this I simply began to say, "OK, please call me next year when you have an opening for a speaker."

Whenever we answer objections in this way, we are doomed to fail. I now know that in a consulting business, the chances of someone rejecting you once and using you later are very low: if they don't use you the first time, you will have a much tougher sale the second and third times. You cannot wait for them to call you. You must keep trying. In effect, I was saying to my prospects, "When you give me a rejection, I think you are giving me conflict." Because of my fear of rejection, I tried to avoid conflict, thereby avoiding any psychological pain if they said or even implied that they didn't like me or my ideas.

## Fear of Rejection Checklist

Below is a checklist, the answers to which will give you a better idea of the degree and amount of rejection you might be experiencing.

- ☐ Do you have trouble closing? Do you let prospects stall you too often?
- ☐ Do you spend too long explaining rather than selling?
- ☐ Are you unable to make consistent daily calls?
- ☐ Do you procrastinate prospecting activity?
- ☐ Do you readily agree with prospects' objections?
- ☐ Do you give in too easily to discount demands?
- ☐ Does your heart rate quicken, do your hands get clammy, and does your perspiration level increase during prospecting calls?
- ☐ Do you find it difficult to introduce yourself to strangers?
- ☐ Do you experience anxiety when asking for appointments?
- ☐ Do you experience difficulty asking for referrals?

If you answered yes to any three of these questions, you may be experiencing a secondary, or even in some rare cases a primary, fear of rejection.

## Coping with Fear of Rejection

Here are three tips to help you begin to overcome with a fear of rejection:

1. Introduce yourself to at least one person—a stranger—every day this week. Those of us with an intense fear of rejection dislike meeting people we don't know because it is uncomfortable, but also because they may display a lack of interest in us. But by putting yourself forward and saying, for example, "My name is Kerry Johnson. I would like to meet you," we will more often than not find that they are as interested in talking to us as we are to them.

   Yes, we may experience suspicion on their part. People often are not friendly enough to introduce themselves to others when there is no apparent reason to do so. But they typically will quickly both acknowledge our introduction and be grateful for it.

2. Try to trial-close at least one prospect each day next week. By this I mean saying to a prospect something like, "John, how do you like this idea so far?" or "Nancy, does this solution seem like the right way to go?" You should trial-close in a way that is most appropriate for your business.

   People with a fear of rejection typically have extreme difficulty closing simply because they perceive that the relation is being cut off if the prospect says no. Remember, however, that some sales require a very long cycle, so the amount of time spent in developing the relationship—replete with its initial nos—is a worthwhile investment of time.

For people who experience severe fear of rejection, this initial period of investing time when the prospect is saying no is almost like trying to kiss a girl who is leaning backwards. There is no fulfillment.

3. Try to negotiate for something that you thought was nonnegotiable. Everything is negotiable. Recent self-help books drive home this simple fact: nothing is ironclad. Whether it be groceries, dry goods, or hotel rooms, if you can talk to the manager or decision maker, you are very likely to negotiate a better deal.

   Recently, I was in Dulles Airport in Washington D.C. I had a ticket to fly on United Airlines to Los Angeles. But I was two hours early for my flight. I looked around the terminal and noticed on a video screen that American Airlines had an earlier flight to LA. I walked up to the American ticket agent with my United ticket and said, "If you let me fly first-class on your flight, I'll give you the business instead of United."

   To my surprise, I had gotten very lucky and was talking to the right person. The chief ticket agent said, "We don't normally do this, but the flight is not full tonight. Here's your first-class ticket. Go right on board." Even things that appear to be nonnegotiable are almost always negotiable. That ticket agent could have easily said no to me, and I might have felt a little bit silly for asking. I risked feeling rejected and decided to try to negotiate.

Try to negotiate for something at least once every day for the next week. Don't be afraid of experiencing rejection.

# Four

# Self-Sabotaging Fear Number Two: Fear of Embarrassment

The second self-sabotaging fear that can limit our success is fear of embarrassment. Like fear of rejection, it is characterized by our need to have others like us, respect us, and enjoy our company.

Fear of embarrassment is different from fear of rejection, however, in that even though inside ourselves we experience the fear, we may often try to appear to others—in almost all situations—as totally competent, alert, and bright. Fear of embarrassment involves our ego, self-esteem, and self-confidence.

Sigmund Freud, the father of psychoanalysis, based much of his research on a three-letter word that is a basic source of our fear of embarrassment. Can you guess what it is? If you thought *sex*, you're wrong. It's *ego*.

Although Freud spent a lot of time investigating the sexual reasons for underlying behavior patterns, he surmised that a male might still, even as an adult, secretly be in conflict with his father or his father's influence. (In adult life, father figures could take the form of your superior at work or even a domineering spouse.) A male wants his own identity, but realizes that his father is sharper because he is older and therefore has more experience. The male fears his father will catch him making an embarrassing error and call him "stupid," or say, "You don't know what you're talking about."

Every time a male hears verbal abuse from his father, or someone who reminds him of his father, he experiences a feeling of embarrassment and even a loss of self-esteem, but the real problem resides within his ego.

Males spend lifetimes trying to build their egos up. Often they live in mortal fear that someone might embarrass them and tear their egos to shreds.

In your day-to-day conversations, how often do you hear people protect themselves from the fear of embarrassment by saying things like, "I'm sure you know much more about this than I do" or "I could very well be wrong, but . . ."? Such statements are unconscious attempts to admit ignorance before the fact, just in case we turn out to be mistaken. "I'll give you my opinion, but don't hold me to it." If we claim ignorance in advance, there is less chance we will make an embarrassing mistake.

Many salespeople find it difficult to sell new ideas or new products because of a fear of embarrassment. "What if my prospect asks me something about this product I can't answer? I'll look foolish." Or they punish themselves by coming out of an interview thinking, "What a stupid thing to say. Why did I say that?"

If they dwell on the potential to make mistakes and embarrass themselves, they may become too tentative in dealing with prospects and ultimately lose sales.

A sales manager once told me about a producer who avoided making prospecting calls. Instead the salesman would spend almost all of his time studying the products. He would bring mountains of brochures, handouts, and printouts containing product information on a sales call. Whenever a prospect asked a question of the salesman, although he knew the answer, the salesman would avoid the chance of being wrong by looking up the answer in his reference materials. Unfortunately, this is both a poor way to sell and a great way to lose spontaneity and rapport with a prospect.

The sharpest, most successful salespeople bring in technical assistance only if needed, in the form of a third-party expert. When a tough question comes up, they'll defer to the expert. These big hitters are not embarrassed that the expert may have more expertise than them. They don't want to look foolish but also realize they can't know everything. These superstars are the first to say, "I don't try to learn everything. I go out and get my feet wet, but I don't overlearn the product."

We must study our products or services, but if we are in sales, we should not let this dominate our activity.

## Sell What They Need, Not How It Works

Fear of embarrassment manifests in salespeople who feel the need to educate others rather than sell the prospect. They wrongly assume they can overcome their fear of embarrassment by impressing the prospect into respecting his or her level of knowledge. They irrationally hope that the prospect will say, "I'll buy from you because you're so smart. You know more about the product than anyone I've seen."

I have to admit that I've never bought anything from the most technically competent salesperson I could find. I mostly buy from the salesperson who can find out what I need and sell it to me. If this were not true of most prospects, technical experts would be the most successful salespeople. There would be no need for sales skills.

I recently bought another computer. A laptop seemed to be what I needed. So I went to a discount computer store and asked a salesman to help me. He must have had a deep fear of embarrassment. Although he did finally ask me what I needed, he wasted at least an hour of my time lecturing me about chip speech, video-card responsiveness, and memory partitioning. I'm sure he thought I would be impressed by his technical brilliance. I'm also sure he felt a little foolish in a sales situation and tried to make up for it by reciting a 500-page brief on how computers operate.

The situation reminded me of the child who asked his father where he came from. Thinking the time was right, the father proceeded to recite the birds-and-bees version of human reproduction for forty-five minutes. Afterward, the father asked the boy if he had any further questions. Looking bored, the little boy said, "Jimmy said he came from Cincinnati. I just wanted to know where I came from."

## Overcoming Intimidation

I often meet people suffering from fear of embarrassment who use very advanced avoidance behaviors. They are experts at putting off uncomfortable situations in which they could experience embarrassment. When they are asked why they're not prospecting to a specific market such as to doctors, lawyers, or top executives, they are likely to say things like, "I'll prospect that market after I finish my MBA." or "I'll prospect that business owner after I get my CLU (chartered life underwriter)."

Do you fear talking to people who may know more than you do? Or who may intimidate you?

Not long ago, I spoke to an insurance agent who told me he and a client had gone to an accountant to try to find out how suitable an insurance product the agent had suggested for his client might actually be. The accountant not only gave it thumbs-down, but said that insurance was a lousy product to buy in a highly inflationary, volatile economy. The agent was so affected by that experience that he made a pact with himself then and there to never again deal with accountants.

Why would this happen? The agent didn't feel as technically competent as the accountant. The CPA displayed his technical expertise by quoting from numerous legal statutes and accounting codes. The agent simply felt foolish and was embarrassed in front of his client.

The fear of embarrassment often plagues newer salespeople. Young producers are often asked by their prospects how long they have been in the business or how much experience they have. As a result of their fear of embarrassment, new salespeople may even lie to cover their lack of experience.

A few years ago, a new financial-products salesman told me he had exaggerated to a prospect the number of years' experience he had selling his product. Unfortunately, the prospect met the salesman's boss after a few months. When they discussed the salesman, the discussion led to experience. As you may have guessed, the salesman lost his client. The salesman told me he learned a very costly lesson. The temptation to lie to avoid appearing foolish is very high. If you are working with new salespeople, help them see how valuable they are with their current level of skill and experience. Help them focus on what they do know rather than what they don't.

Many people don't feel adequate until they earn an advanced degree. A designation such as CPA, CLU, CFP or a degree such as MBA or PhD may indicate an advanced level of extra education. This may have been obtained to serve as a psychological crutch in order to rationalize a way out of situations in which the person may not feel confident.

Fear of embarrassment is a fear that others may not respect you in the way you want. We often try to justify to ourselves why we weren't successful in a sales or negotiation situation. We rationalize in order to take the burden of failure and responsibility off our shoulders. We determine we can't possibly be successful because of a corollary to fear of embarrassment called *intimidation*.

I had a conversation with a man who was running for a school-board election but was clearly intimidated by his opponent. He decided midway through the election that he didn't want to campaign anymore. He told me his opponent had a PhD in education and probably knew more about the education problems affecting the school system. Besides that, he rationalized that he really couldn't put the needed hours into making the school board more effective, and that in thinking about it, it just wasn't something he felt he wanted.

This is a good example of how intimidation or fear of embarrassment makes us rationalize why we don't become successful or why we can't achieve something we want. It's basically an attempt to avoid people who may know more than you or who have rejected you in the past.

I played tennis in college. Shortly before I went to the Grand Prix tennis tour, I had the opportunity to play a friendly game in La Jolla, California, with a man in his late fifties. He had a very soft serve, but he was like a backboard. He could hit everything back.

A tremendous player for his age, I found myself getting upset at not being able to return his soft underspins and slices effectively. I wasn't able to hit any winners or put the ball away. I got mad at his ability to return so many shots to me. He beat me in three sets.

As I drove home, I remember making a promise to myself that I would never play older players again. I foolishly rationalized that hitting with pushers was probably just hurting my game. It would spoil my game, much as playing racketball might spoil a tennis player's timing.

This is a typical example of the fear of embarrassment. I had decided that, rather than risk being embarrassed again, I would never put myself in a similar situation, even though the fact that he was older had nothing to do with his beating me. I let the fact that he was an older player who beat me intimidate me so much that I wouldn't play anyone similar again.

## Leaping the Barrier

If you have a fear of embarrassment, you probably recognize some of the symptoms just discussed. Of course, this does not mean you are incompetent or won't be able to do a good job at selling or dealing with your clients. It merely means there is a barrier keeping you from achieving what you want.

Your fear of embarrassment puts a limitation on your overall productivity. Fear of embarrassment may be unconsciously motivating you to keep out of situations in which you may not feel as competent or as respected as you want to be.

Henry Ford was once questioned about his technical expertise in a courtroom hearing. He was even queried about his abilities and sophistication in leading a major corporation. When asked "What is single-line depreciation in accounting?" Ford, the eighth-grade dropout, responded, "I don't know."

"Mr. Ford, how many tires do you buy each year?"

"I don't know," responded Ford.

"Mr. Ford," the questioner asked, "Who was the third president of the United States?"

Ford replied, "I don't know, and I don't care. I'm not paid to be a damn encyclopedia. I surround myself with experts to give me the facts. I'm paid millions of dollars each year to put these facts together effectively."

Obviously Henry Ford didn't have a fear of embarrassment.

One of the most famous people to openly admit a fear of embarrassment was Jim Hart, former quarterback for the St. Louis Cardinals football team. After speaking at a sales conference in Cape Girardeau, Missouri, Jim told me of a very embarrassing experience. The Cardinals played the Los Angeles Rams. The Rams had a superstar defensive lineman by the name of Merlin Olson. Merlin was one of the most aggressive defensive linemen in football at that time.

It was third and long. Hart dropped back in the pocket to pass. His favorite wide receiver went deep. The Rams put on a strong rush. He saw Olson toss his own offensive linemen in the air like volleyballs.

Waiting a few moments longer, Hart finally cocked his arm, attempting to throw the longest touchdown pass of his career. Suddenly, before the ball release, Olson tackled Hart from his blind side. Hart felt a freight train hit his back and force him face down into the turf. Olson not only knocked Hart to the ground, but because of his momentum, kept pushing Hart across the natural turf so fervently that Hart's trousers filled up with about four pounds of soil in a very embarrassing location.

Realizing he couldn't reach into his pants in front of 40,000 stadium spectators, he walked backed to his huddle. He explained the problem to his teammates. He requested that the players tightly enclose him in the huddle so that he could reach into his pants and pull out the dirt.

His teammates complied, and the huddle gathered more tightly. Just as Jim Hart put his hands into his pants to pull the dirt out, his teammates scattered, leaving Hart the focal point of 40,000 spectators.

Like Jim Hart, after you have a very embarrassing experience, you may develop a fear that leads you to avoid situations that may make you feel foolish. Or you might want to avoid people who think they know more than you. Giving speeches to people you don't know might seem impossible to someone experiencing a severe case of fear of embarrassment.

Speaking in front of a group is said to scare most Americans even more than death itself. I was in Las Vegas giving a speech recently when a speaker followed me on the topic of speaking in front of groups. He said, "The biggest fear we have is speaking to a group. The next biggest fear is dying. The third biggest fear is dying while speaking in front of a group."

We are so frightened of what people may think of us that we avoid baring our souls in speeches for fear of what a listener might think. But if your prospects don't hear you, there's little chance they'll buy from you.

## Seminar Selling

If you have a fear of embarrassment, you may not be willing to engage in what is one of the best marketing strategies available. This strategy has led to numerous overnight sales successes. It works simply because through it you can prospect fifty people in the time it ordinarily takes to prospect one. Since it is very high-touch, it is far better than media or social advertising and is almost as effectiveness as a one-to-one meeting.

This advanced concept is called *seminar selling*. It is one of the hottest sales strategies around. It is hard not to find a seminar advertisement in your daily newspaper. Most of these presentations make lots of money.

There's an easy way to get started in the seminar market. Tom Brinker, who had been a moderately successful financial-services salesman in Pittsburgh, took my suggestions. He started out simply and slowly by speaking to service clubs like Rotary, Lions, and Kiwanis. His topic was straightforward: "How to Save Money at Tax Time." At first Tom spoke at least once a week. As he became comfortable, he increased the frequency of his presentations to professional associations.

Tom doubled his business almost overnight. His audiences felt so motivated from his presentations that they would go up to him afterwards, hand him their business cards, and ask him to call.

From this point on, Tom was on a fast track to sales success. Tom was asked to be a guest on a Philadelphia radio show on personal finance. A few weeks later, he was asked to be a regular guest, and he now has his own show.

Can you guess what would happen if you could ask a prospect to tune in to your weekly radio show? What a credibility boost! Tom has built his business simply by doing the right things correctly. He started by having a desire to get over his fear of embarrassment and ended by quadrupling his business through seminar-selling techniques.

## Five Steps to Great Seminar Presentations

If you want to prospect fifty people in the time it takes to prospect one, follow these steps. But before you do, remember: great speakers are made, not born. Most speakers worth their salt have survived one disastrous speaking engagement after another as they learned how to be effective in front of a group. Those of us who have overcome the fear of embarrassment to become effective speakers have a motto for new speakers entering the fray: "Either you have bombed or you will bomb."

Ideally, with a little study, you can temper that awful experience. Here are the five steps that will help make your seminar message so full of impact that your listeners will ask you to do business with them.

1. Ask a rhetorical question of the group and then pause. You'll get a number of important benefits from using this technique: You will grab the group's attention by asking them to think about an answer. You also let them know you will be solving a problem. Asking an initial rhetorical question is one of the best ways for a speaker to generate an audience's interest.

   During one of my presentations, I asked the rhetorical question, "How many of you have had trouble getting through to a prospect?"

   Without exception, not only do the attendees raise their hands, but, in unison, they also say yes as their response. The audience immediately senses a benefit to be gained by listening to my presentation. An old adage in speaking suggests that if you don't grab the audience in the first five minutes, you may lose them until the last five minutes, when they sense that you are almost finished.

2. Use your own personal experiences to illustrate your points. Most groups don't want a book report by an amateur when an expert is readily available. If you give the audience the sense that you have lived the concepts you are preaching, their interest will be piqued. You'll keep their attention much longer.

   In a presentation I gave a few years ago, I discussed fear of success. As an illustration, I talked about one of my past professional tennis matches. I played in Rome, Italy, in 1977 against their national tennis champion in the Italian Open. In the second set, the Italian fans, sensing that their hometown champion was losing, threw lire coins down on the stadium's clay court. The umpire postponed the match until the lire were cleared from the surface. Jubilant that I was finally getting paid, I sat down next to my doubles partner and bragged that the Italian tennis spectators were so enthralled with my playing that they threw money in appreciation.

   My partner told me that they fans were not showing appreciation; the lire coins they were throwing were practically worthless. Instead they were communicating an old Italian warning: If I beat their hometown boy, I would not make it out of the parking lot. That brought on a big case of fear of success.

   By illustrating the fear of success with a personal anecdote, I gave the audience a part of myself. Share your personality in your presentations. Audiences put as much value in this as they do in your content. Besides arousing and increasing the group's interest, you help them grasp your concepts and understand more quickly.

3. Get the audience to participate. Conference attendees are tired of being lectured to or talked at. They want to be involved. They want to be part of the program. One reason teleconferencing has not totally taken over meetings, according to *Megatrends* author John Naisbitt, is that it is not high-touch enough. When a group is assembled, they want more involvement than just watching a live version of a video presentation. They want to experience it.

   There are many ways of helping a group experience a presentation. One of the best is to intermittently call audience members up to the front of the room. In a presentation I do called "How to Read Your Client's Mind," I bring at least four people, one at a time throughout the program, to the front of the room to illustrate my concepts. Nothing will do more to increase your listeners' attention than to watch one of their own participating in the program.

   Get the group to raise their hands in response to questions. Better yet, shed the security of the podium and walk among the audience as you speak. Oprah Winfrey, in her popular talk show, made a career of walking among the audience, microphone in hand. Granted, Winfrey ensured that questions were fielded to the guests, but she did involve her audience in the whole process. Her success was phenomenal—the waiting list for Winfrey's studio audience list was months long.

   Get a roving microphone and walk among your group. You don't need notes. Why not jot down one-word memory joggers and leave them on a front-row seat? No one will sit in the front row anyway.

   Call audience members by name. Learn a dozen or so of your audience members' names. Call them out every so often. Every attendee will think you also know his or her name.

4. Use humor to conclude every major point. Johnny Carson once said that people will pay much more to be entertained than they will to be educated. There's quite a bit of truth to his comment. In memory retention studies done at San Diego State University, researchers found that when ideas are associated with humor, they are not only remembered longer but retained with much more detail than ideas presented without humor. While you are not likely to be an aspiring comedian, a touch of humor enhances any message you give. Your attendees basically want to enjoy or feel good about your speech, no matter what the topic. When you use humor, you break down suspicion, get rid of skepticism, and remove other psychological barriers that prevent your listeners from accepting your ideas.

   I recently spoke at the annual convention of the International Association for Financial Planning. My presentation was jam-packed with very sophisticated client-relations research. Nonetheless, I pumped humor in about every four to five minutes. Not only did the audience respond, but afterwards numerous attendees told me that they came to my program because they heard it was fun.

   I recommend that you weave one-liners into your personal stories. If they help illustrate your point, you'll be evaluated not only as a good speaker, but also as a charismatic one. Charismatic speakers make an audience feel good as well as give valuable content.

   A great place to get humorous one-liners is from local comedy nightclubs. I get a lot of good ideas for humor from the young comedians who perform at these clubs. I then adapt the humor for my own use.

Another great place to get humor is from Bob Orben's series of books on humor for speakers. His *Two Thousand Sure-Fire Jokes for Speakers: The Encyclopedia of One-Liner Comedy* and *The Ad-Libber's Handbook* include some of the funniest topical one-liners I have ever read.

5. Never present more than four or five major ideas at any one sitting. Inexperienced speakers simply try to cram too much into a very short time period. They end up treating their subject very superficially. Avoid this mistake. The mind can absorb only what the seat can endure. The seat will endure a lot more if you properly present only four or five major ideas at a time. Of course, the length of time you speak depends on the entertainment value. I'm often asked how long one should speak before a break.

   A good rule of thumb, if you're using my five steps, is to speak no more than ninety minutes without a break. If you are not using my steps, twenty to thirty minutes is about the maximum.

**Remember these five steps for effective speaking.**

Step 1. Ask a rhetorical question of the group and then pause.

Step 2. Use your own personal experiences to illustrate your points.

Step 3. Get the audience to participate.

Step 4. Use humor to conclude every major point.

Step 5. Never present more than four or five major ideas at any one sitting.

A financial planner in Detroit, Michigan, uses seminar selling every month or two. He conducts public seminars on how a middle-income earner can make money on investments. While he is not a gifted speaker, he has learned to overcome his fear of embarrassment. He has learned that from every 100 attendees, forty to fifty will become his clients. His average client invests $300,000. All this from a technique most salespeople are too often afraid to try.

Promise yourself that in the next month you will stand up in front of at least one group of strangers and discuss your business. Afterward, ask for business cards for follow-up. Use the speaking ideas outlined in this chapter to overcome your fear of embarrassment.

Though we might try to deny it, remember that we all face potentially embarrassing situations. Relax: we live through them. During a recent seminar, I asked for a show of hands from those who had absolutely no fear of embarrassment. One very proud male said he never had and never will have a fear of embarrassment. I then said, "Pretend for a moment that you took some great clients to a very posh dinner in a very swanky restaurant. During dinner, you decide to use the restaurant's plush restroom. Unfortunately, you splash some water on your trousers about waist level. If you have no fear of embarrassment, why do you pull your pants up to the hot-air dryer for thirty minutes until the trousers dry? Then, as you rejoin your party, you look back and discover you've been trailing toilet paper for thirty feet. Who wouldn't be embarrassed by that situation?"

# Five

# Self-Sabotaging Fear Number Three: Fear of Failure

Do you find yourself unwilling to take a risk on a new idea or method of doing business?

Do you find yourself wanting to stay with a sure thing that you rarely change, or staying with a product you've sold for years rather than try something new and different?

Do you find increasing difficulty in setting goals for even a month, let alone a year or five years, down the road?

Do you find it difficult to take others' advice? And even though the advice is good, do you find it tough to use it promptly in your business?

These are all symptoms of another limitation to your success and productivity: *fear of failure*.

Fear of failure may be a protection device for avoiding potentially disastrous situations. More often than not, it is irrational and arises when we wonder what may happen if we fail. Its source is our own insecurity. As a great philosopher once said, "Worry is merely the interest paid now on trouble that is not yet due."

## Entrepreneurial Risk Taking

Obviously if we don't take risks, we can't fail. If we don't stick our necks out, we will never get them chopped off. We also will never have to face our fear of failure head-on. But then again, we'll probably never have any great success either.

As an entrepreneur, I've often asked myself, "Why do so few people take risks that could make them millions of dollars? Why are there so few rags-to-riches stories? And why do so many people stay in jobs they hate or in relationships they dislike year after year?"

These individuals fear taking risks or making changes. They suffer from fear of failure. Usually their thoughts run something like this: "What will happen if I don't make it? What will happen to me if my expectations don't work out?" They rationalize so that they will not have to risk failure.

If we tell someone we are going to do something and we don't follow through, then in a sense we've failed. Or at least we're likely to feel that we've failed and that this person we've shared our goal with will think poorly of us.

## Avoiding Commitments

Many people have learned to avoid failure by avoiding public commitments. A short time ago I heard a story about a manager who was with a salesperson. The manager said, "I need to know what your goals are for this year."

The salesperson responded, "I don't believe in that stuff. Don't write anything down for me."

The manager said, "The company requires that I put something down."

"Well, put down last year's goal minus 10 percent. I don't believe in that garbage anyway."

"What do you mean?" said the manager. "We paid a motivational speaker $5,000 to pump you people up. Do you remember what he said? Be positive, positive, positive. Did you hear him speak?"

"Yes, sir, I did."

"What do you have to say now?"

"I'm positive I can't make my goals this month."

Will Rogers once said, "Even though you're on the right track, you'll get run over if you don't move fast enough." But very often fear-of-failure people don't move fast enough because they're afraid to make a commitment. They fear what will happen if they aren't able to live up to it. By not publicly committing ourselves, we could feel that we are not accountable. Later on, we don't have to explain or rationalize why we may not have fulfilled our promise.

## Avoiding Failure at All Costs

The roots of the fear of failure are similar to those of many other fears. We have been socialized by our parents and peers to avoid failure at all costs. We are rewarded for hitting a home run, but criticized for striking out. A child feels inadequate when he doesn't bring home straight As or isn't elected president of the student body.

The fear of failure has some interesting similarities to the fear of embarrassment. Often, like those who suffer from fear of embarrassment, fear-of-failure people tend to rationalize why they didn't achieve success: "I could have won that sales competition, but decided it wasn't worth it, so I quit midway through," or "I didn't really want that account or that policy anyway. I think the buyer would have been too tough to work with."

People suffering from either the fear of failure or the fear of embarrassment tend to have very low self-esteem and self-confidence. They might tell us how great they are or how easily they sold a house or a million-dollar policy. But they often can't feel worthwhile unless they're able to achieve some great business or personal success, like winning a golf tournament, buying a Rolls-Royce, or selling a million-dollar account.

Even with self-confidence problems, fear-of-failure individuals need not worry, because they can learn to deal with their fears. They can take this self-sabotaging behavior, toss it right out the window, and open up a whole new door to productivity and profitability.

## How Fear of Failure Kills Production

Not only does fear of failure sabotage behavior, it is probably one of the most insidious fears that most salespeople or managers face and that limit their productivity.

Fear of failure stems from focusing more on the downside—the negative risk of taking chances—than on the upside potential. Yet in case after case, we witness entrepreneurs like Steve Jobs, founder of Apple Inc., taking risks early on, not concentrating on the negative chances of failing. What's the result of taking chances? Jobs, with the help of partner Steve Wozniak, started a corporation destined to become one of the highest-growth companies in the United States.

In an interview, when asked about the risk he took, Jobs simply said he had nothing to lose compared to the benefits he could gain.

To have such an attitude is more easily said than done. Most Americans are still conditioned to receiving a regular, guaranteed income from the paycheck from their 8-to-5 jobs.

To some societies, the idea of taking a risk would be shocking. One of the few societies with guaranteed employment is Japan, where many workers are practically promised they will never be fired. The idea of taking a risk to the average Japanese worker is as foreign as American-made computers.

It probably would have helped us if, as children, we had been pushed to take more risks. But we can't change the past.

In the early 1980s, my father, Bill Johnson, one of the art directors for Crown-Zellerbach Paper Corporation, was caught up in a corporate reorganization. The company that purchased Crown-Zellerbach decided it had too many layers of midlevel managers, precisely the area in which my father worked. My father was given a choice. At fifty-two years old, he was asked either to take early retirement at full pay for three years or stay with the company and be demoted to commercial artist with a pay decrease. He called me one day and said, "I don't know what to do. I've got two choices, and frankly, I'm worried about my future." I said, "Dad, this is a no-brainer. You've got a choice of going on early retirement with full pay or staying there with less money and a demotion. What is there to think about?"

There was no question that this was the perfect opportunity for my father to leave and go out on his own. For years he had wanted to start his own graphic-design corporation. He always wanted to be a business owner, but because of family responsibilities, he was never able to take advantage of his ambition. His risk tolerance was low. But here he was presented with an opportunity for a guaranteed income for three years while he started up his own firm—virtually a wide-open door to guaranteed success. It made my father nervous. He still worried about failing when he was practically guaranteed protection from any downside risk.

My father had been protected financially for many years with a guaranteed paycheck, so even though he was offered a plum opportunity, his fear of failure was pervasive. It wasn't until I pointed this out that he was able to overcome his fear of failure and successfully start his own firm.

## How to Tackle Fear of Failure Head-On

If you are experiencing fear of failure, here are three things you can do to tackle the fear head-on.

1. In the next couple of days, take some little risks or face a challenge, knowing full well that failure could be impending.

   Play a card game at which you are not proficient. Try to get in some minor competition with your spouse—perhaps something as simple as who can memorize more words in a row. Engage yourself in a competitive task at which you could fail. While this is not nearly as risky as putting $10,000 into a highly volatile stock on the New York Stock Exchange, it will weaken your phobia about failure and give you a place to start.

   Another idea might be to set a goal such as making a few extra prospecting phone calls. You may know full well you might not have time to make those calls, but take the risk. Promise yourself you will make them anyway. Then try to live up to the promise.

2. Engage in sports competition. Sports are a great practice ground for helping us deal with our fear of failure. In all sports,

any time there is competition, there is always a chance to fail. Whether you are bowling, golfing, or playing tennis, there is always someone out there who could bury you in the dust.

I travel coast-to-coast about 8,000 miles a week. (This is not a lot of miles when you consider how far my baggage travels.) I still enjoy playing tennis, but because of my pro tennis background, hosts at conventions have high expectations of seeing me play an excellent game. Because I'm very rusty and out of practice, I often try to avoid playing tennis on the road for fear that I might be beaten by a lesser player.

Lately I've even made a conscious effort to play against people I know can beat me, only because I enjoy playing so much. This may seem like an inconsequential competition to you, but to an ex–pro tennis player who has a big ego, it could result in a serious loss of self-esteem.

Try to engage yourself in a sports competition in which you expect to win but where there is some chance you could lose.

3. Next time you have a setback in a job or task, tell somebody else in your business or even a close associate about your failure. Fear-of-failure people often avoid admitting their failures to anyone. They are so distraught by their setbacks that they hesitate to let others know of their own self-perceived weakness. By admitting your failure to others, you will realize that others have been in exactly the same place you are.

We often think of failure as having a worse sting than it really does. There is a fantasy of impending doom. When people have aspirations of starting major corporations, there is always the chance they could lose everything, including their homes and all their assets. But even with failure, entrepreneurs often bounce back and admit that failing wasn't nearly as bad as they expected it to be.

Do these three activities during the next seven days. While they may not stop your fear of failure flat, they will give you a few tools to help deal more effectively with it.

# Six

# Self-Sabotaging Fear Number Four: Fear of Success

The fourth self-sabotaging fear that limits our performance and productivity is fear of success. Of all the fears we may have, this is one of the least understood but can be one of the most disastrous. It prevents us from reaching our maximum potential and producing as much as we can.

Fear-of-success sufferers think they shouldn't be doing as well as they're doing right now. They may believe they've been too successful too fast. They'd actually feel better if their success would just slow down a bit. They tend to have thoughts like these adages:

*It's more difficult to stay on a fast horse than a slow one.*

*Be wary of too much too fast.*

*There's no such thing as a free lunch.*

They tell themselves, "This just can't last." Achieving a lot of success very quickly sincerely makes fear-of-success sufferers just plain uncomfortable.

While many individuals—including some psychologists—think of fear of success as basically a confidence or self-esteem problem, it's really more deeply rooted than that. It results from having a preconceived notion of just how difficult things are or how tough it is to succeed.

When we don't meet problems we expected, we achieve more and produce faster. At first we feel happy and have a great sense of accomplishment. But gradually, if we're suffering from the fear of success, we become anxious and sometimes even upset. Psychologically we are unprepared to deal with this sudden onset of success. We have too much success too fast.

## Symptoms of Fear of Success

I'm often asked what the symptoms are of fear of success. While they vary, the experience is generally similar to that of a real-estate agent I met recently who told me he used to get a great deal of business by using direct mail. He had used direct mail for more than one year, but then he stopped. I commented, "It's too bad it didn't work for you." He said, "No, it did work. In fact, the effort pulled in at least a 35 percent increase in my business that year." I asked, "Why did you stop?" He didn't know. It worked too well for him. In fact, it worked so well it made him uncomfortable. It gave him too much success.

You are more than likely suffering from the fear of success if you find yourself with any of these symptoms:

Do you find that your business is not growing nearly as fast as it once did?

Are you failing to follow up on the leads or referrals you get?

When you know you should follow up by telephone after a direct mailing for the best results, are you not doing so?

Fear of success sabotages our productivity. Last year I worked with a bright, motivated salesperson who sabotaged her own productivity for this reason. She was new to sales. As a schoolteacher, she had made $44,000 a year. In her first six months as a salesperson, she made $41,000. What did she make in the last six months of the year? You guessed it—$3,000.

I spoke recently with a salesperson who was a great producer but had switched jobs a lot in a short time. Each time he reached the level where he was tagged to be promoted to sales manager, he would quit. While he made it clear to friends and coworkers that he aspired to be a manager, when the opportunity arose, he ran away from it. He seemed afraid of the responsibility.

Both of these salespeople, in shying away from responsibility, exhibited symptoms typical of fear of success.

We have all either experienced the fear of success ourselves or met people who do. Why do so many people I meet tell me they were four units short of a college degree when they dropped out? Why do so many playwrights disappear after opening night?

## Childhood Roots

Like the other self-sabotaging fears, fear of success usually stems from our youth and the messages we received from our parents.

When I was eight years old, I remember spending a whole day building a wooden go-cart. It was rickety and ugly. But I thought it looked like a Formula 1 Racer. I proudly showed it to my father who commented, "When you get older, I'll show you how to build a good one." Heartbreak! My father didn't give me any praise and encouragement for all my work and effort. The sense of accomplishment and the success I experienced building that cart suddenly didn't seem all that important.

As children, we may have been given conflicting messages about success. Did your parents ever tell you things like these?

"You're too smart for your own good" (But you had better bring back a good report card.)

"Don't be a show-off." (But you had better be a standout if you want to get somewhere.)

"Money is the root of all evil." (But get out there, kid, and make those bucks.)

Such negative criticism, coupled with conflicting messages, not only causes confusion, but also leaves us feeling, "Even if I succeed, it's not good enough."

The roots of our fear of success could indeed stem from our upbringing. Probably our parents were middle-class, raising you with belief systems and attitudes typical of that socioeconomic status (SES). As long as we stay within the set SES boundaries we were brought up with, all is well. But when our success moves us beyond our SES walls, we may begin to experience discomfort.

Success may not be what we actually fear. The trappings of success may be what frightens us. In *The Beverly Hillbillies*, a popular 1960s television show, Granny constantly made demands on her son-in-law, Jed, to go back to their home in the Ozarks. She was so uncomfortable with her newfound state of wealth that she turned their Beverly Hills mansion into a backwoods shack, whiskey still and all. Because Jed's daughter, Ellie-May, and their cousin Jethro were in a sense still growing up and had not developed fixed notions about their proper socioeconomic status, they loved the new surroundings. They were learning to feel comfortable with their wealth and how to act with a great deal of money.

## Sheer Discomfort

Why do the rich stay rich and the poor stay poor? The answer lies in comfort levels. In the late 1970s, the Carter administration poured millions of dollars into slum renovations, turning several New York City tenement slums into high-rise dwellings. What are they now? High-rise slums!

Our family's level of affluence is likely to be the level with which we feel most comfortable. When we experience the fear of success, we may be sabotaging our chances to make a higher income because of the sheer discomfort a change in lifestyle would bring.

Surprising as it might seem, most of us make within 10 to 20 percent of our best friend's income. What would happen if our income doubled this year? We could buy a house in a more affluent area, buy new cars, even go on an extended vacation. But our friends probably wouldn't have the funds to share those experiences.

Going to a higher socioeconomic status might entail making new friends and losing old ones. Many of us would rather keep our old friends than try to cope with financial prosperity and its accompanying changes.

Recently during a consulting project for a real-estate company, I encountered a salesperson who had too much business. An axiom of the consulting industry is that you can never have too much business. Once you reach the capacity of your staff and resources, you hire and train more people to take on the added work. Simple as this seems, the realtor's excuse for not attending a necessary educational mortgage-financing conference was, "I've already got enough business. I don't need to attend." I laughed and said, "Jack Welch, past CEO of General Electric, never said he had too much business, and neither do you."

What she was really saying was, "I'm uncomfortable with my high success. I don't want to get in any deeper." She viewed success as troublesome. For her it might have seemed a misfortune rather than a blessing. Top salespeople in the real-estate industry will often start up their own companies when they have more business than they can handle. But this woman seemed to fear the added responsibility of expanding her success.

Fear of success may come from feeling that we are not as deserving as others. In many cases, the fear of success stems from our admiration, respect, or even awe for a boss, parents, or a mentor. We may feel, "He taught me everything I know. He's much more perceptive and intelligent than I could ever be." But suddenly you find yourself making more money or achieving greater success than that person. We begin to question our success.

The ultimate fear of success results in suicide. Freddie Prinze, the young comedian, committed suicide largely because of his discomfort with success. He spent hundreds of thousands of dollars on elaborate, expensive gifts for his parents, seemingly in an effort to relieve his guilt at being so successful. Why did rock stars Elvis Presley, Janis Joplin, and Kurt Cobain—just at the time when they seemingly had everything—self-destruct and die of drug overdoses? Why did Richard Nixon commit political suicide by not destroying the White House tapes?

## Undeserving of Success

Here's how fear of success can affect us. You're playing golf and about to putt on the eighteenth green. Three of your friends have missed their putts. You realize that if you can sink your one-foot putt, you'll win that beer. You take a couple of practice swings, and suddenly you get a flash. "Hey," you think, "my friends really should be winning. I've never beaten them before. Why am I ahead? I'm not as good as they are." If you have no fear of success, then why does your putt go past the hole, all the way down to the clubhouse?

This could never happen, right? Wrong. In 1984, on the women's tennis tour stop at Amelia Island, Florida, Chris Evert Lloyd was pitted against Carling Bassett. Carling was the darling tennis star from Toronto. Her late wealthy father had been the owner of the Tampa Bay Buccaneers football team. Carling was playing at the top of her game. She had been playing superbly during the whole tournament. But now in the finals, she faced Chris Evert Lloyd. True to her tournament form, Carling soundly trounced Chris in the first set, 6 to 3, and was about to defeat Chris in the second set of the best-of-three-set match. At 5 games to 2, Carling double-faulted her serve. She netted some easy shots, letting Chris back into the match. Chris went on to win the next five games, as well as the set. She defeated Carling in what should have been an upset victory for Carling.

Interviewed afterward, Carling admitted she probably respected Chris a little too much. Carling said she just could not see herself winning. Chris's reputation may have been more invincible than her strokes. Carling beat herself. She sabotaged herself because she believed she didn't deserve to beat Chris Evert Lloyd. She feared success.

Carling Bassett is not the only pro tennis player to have experienced fear of success. Many years ago I had the opportunity to play a great tennis player named Yannick Noah. Yannick was discovered in Africa by Arthur Ashe, a great tennis star of the 1960s and 1970s. Arthur went to a tournament in Africa, looking for an individual whom he could help develop into a world-class star. He didn't care about the player's technique. He wanted to find the player who won the most matches and had a winning instinct.

Arthur was impressed with Yannick when he saw him play in a tournament. He took him to Monaco, where Yannick studied tennis for ten years. I got the chance to play against Yannick Noah when I was in Cannes, in the south of France. He was a tremendously talented and gifted player. But after our match, he confided that he frequently had problems winning matches when he was way ahead. Yannick Noah told me the story of when he came to the United States to play tennis great Stan Smith.

It was a five-set match. Yannick was up 2 sets to love, 5 games to 1 in the third set. In a five-set match, all he needed was 3 sets to win, but he began missing shot after shot, hitting balls out and double-faulting. Stan Smith came back and won the first set, then came back to win another set, and eventually they tied at 5 to 5.

Yannick told me he felt tremendous anxiety and fear. He was upset at himself that he wasn't playing better, but he realized that Stan Smith was winning only because Yannick was choking. Smith went on to beat Yannick 7 to 5 in the fifth set. Yannick was really going through a fear of success. He was a young player, without Stan Smith's level of experience. He believed he had no business out there winning against a player as great as Stan. Psychologically, Yannick knew that he was good. But that day on the court, he feared Stan's reputation much more than his ability.

The same thing often happens in professional golf tournaments,. A fairly easy putt is missed; a drive goes into the nearest pond or sand trap. Some of the best players can't seem to play well and keep their lead when they're ahead. This isn't just choking or simply a lack of concentration. It stems from feeling self-conscious and anxious about doing so well.

Fear of success may come from feeling overly respectful of a job or from feeling that things should be a lot more difficult to accomplish than they seem.

## Performance Plateaus

When we experience the fear of success, we often find we've reached a performance plateau. We may have worked long and hard to increase our productivity, but we might no longer seem to grow and improve as fast as we once did. Even though we loved what we were doing six months ago, our interest and enthusiasm begin to diminish. We begin to take on the avoidance behaviors experienced with other self-sabotaging fears. We might begin finding it difficult to work, so we procrastinate more. In fact, even though fear-of-success sufferers know they should be working, they sometimes will take a month to six weeks off, twice a year.

All of us tend to have plateaus of productivity for a time. But when we reach a plateau, we may find that we do not grow and improve nearly as fast as our experience leads us to predict.

I spoke to an insurance agent who was not achieving as much as he once did, or as motivated about his job as he once was. He took three months off during the year and worked only four- to five-hour days. I asked him why he didn't work harder, and he said he really didn't know.

I dug deeper. I found that he was making $50,000 a year. He had so much talent and drive, I was surprised he wasn't making twice as much. He told me his father was a teacher in a local school district. The son respected the father immensely. But his father only made $50,000 per year. The father sometimes worked eighteen-hour days, read constantly, and worked hard to support the family. The son felt guilty that he was making more money than his father. The son had only a high-school education, while the father had a master's degree. The son felt it wasn't right to be making more money than his father.

To deal with his fear of success, the agent spoke to his father. He found that his father really enjoyed his job. He also realized that money was not an indication of worth or an indication of respect. He tackled his fear of success head-on and proceeded to double his income within two months. The agent now makes $100,000 and grows as fast as you would expect a hard-working, driven, talented insurance agent to grow.

Here's a quick question: If you were a member of the Kennedy, Rothschild, or DuPont families, would you feel comfortable with your income? Chances are you would not. In our youth we are socialized to expect to achieve a specific level of success. For some of us, that level may be well below our potential, but unfortunately we often just stop and hang on.

## Peer Pressure

Fear of success also results from the pressure our friends put on us. People at all income levels try to find friends with equal resources. As I suggested earlier, most of us make within 10 to 20 percent of our best friend's income. This can have a devastating impact on our productivity and success, because if we make substantially more than our friends, they have comparatively less financial freedom than we do. They aren't able to keep up with us. They don't have the same cars or the same houses. They can't take the same vacations.

A year out of college, a friend's business really took off. He sold computers and was a top producer. The rest of us were just getting our feet wet. I was trying to get experience as a stockbroker, and the others were in management training jobs. Gradually the computer sales broker became more and more successful. We saw less and less of him, but we all admired his trappings of wealth. He had a Porsche, a boat, and even a small house. He often said that he missed us, but we just couldn't keep up. He wanted to go skiing every weekend; we couldn't even afford our own skis. He had a hot ski boat; we could barely afford the gas for it. He footed the bill for us a lot of the time, but we all felt awkward taking his charity. Suddenly his production sank. His success dwindled.

Surprisingly, his setbacks didn't seem to faze him. We saw more of him after that and learned that because of his dwindling income, he had to sell his boat and Porsche. Over a beer one night, I asked him why he let it all go. He said he didn't think it was worth all the effort. He missed his friends.

Success had brought on too much change for him. The discomfort of losing friends was worse than the benefits of making more money. He decided to keep his less-moneyed friends and give up some of his success.

A basic problem that causes fear of success is loss of relationships. When you are making substantially more money than your best friends, you may feel your relationships are drifting apart, and you may try to keep them together by putting a lid on your income level. Friends are hard to find and even harder to keep.

When your income goes up much more than your friends' incomes, your interests may change. You might want to be with other people in your income bracket. This can put an incredible amount of pressure on you. You may start feeling depressed and spend less time with friends. Or you may feel classic stress symptoms such as loneliness, lethargy, and lack of motivation. If this is what success brings, you may not want it.

Managers who employ women as salespeople often witness a fear of success in them. I work with a popular cosmetics firm employing 100,000 female salespeople in the United States. A sales director for the company recruits highly successful saleswomen and pays them on a commission basis. These saleswomen often do so well that they quickly outpace their husband's income level. All too often the male resents not only that his wife is away working in the evening, but that her income is greater than his.

A saleswoman in Calgary, Alberta, told me that her husband constantly ridiculed her success as a salesperson. He seemed to feel that it undermined his masculinity. To avoid his barbs, she purposely kept her income level slightly below his. This was a very conscious, albeit unfortunate, form of avoidance, if not an overt fear of success.

## Broadening Horizons

When we make more money than friends or parents, it broadens our horizons. Our financial problems are eliminated, and we begin to have much more freedom to do things and to meet other people with the same interests and desires we have—people who will stimulate us to even bigger and better things.

But any change brings the potential for anxiety or depression. The change process itself is something most of us try to avoid. This is one reason for procrastination: if we procrastinate, we can't make as much money as we're capable of making. By making less money, we avoid any embarrassment about making "too much." We avoid feeling guilty that we're making more than people we respect.

## Learned Helplessness

The question remains: why do people go through life with these self-imposed barriers, these limitations to their own productivity? One answer lies in learned helplessness.

Please take out a piece of paper. With a pencil or pen, write your name on the top. In sixty seconds, using the same hand that you used to write your name, write your name down the page as many times as you can. Now, with your other hand, please write your name on the top of the paper again. Then for the next sixty seconds, use this other hand to write your name down the page as many times as you can. When you were writing your name with the hand you don't normally write with, did you feel you couldn't do it? Did you feel it was ridiculous even to try? If you answered yes, this is learned helplessness.

Just as we readily learned how to speak and to drive a car, most of us learned equally well what we *can't* do. After knocking our heads against a wall a number of times, we stop and believe whatever we're trying to do is impossible. More importantly, we develop a self-sabotaging barrier or fear.

A few years ago, the University of Minnesota School of Psychology did an interesting experiment. In the Great Lakes region, pike are very numerous. Pike are midsized predators that eat other fish. In the Great Lakes Region, their main prey is minnows.

Two researchers did an experiment in which they put one pike and some minnows into a small aquarium. As expected, the pike promptly devoured the minnows. In the second part of the experiment, the pike was separated from the minnows by a glass barrier. As you might have expected, the pike hit the barrier with its nose time and time again, until after about fifteen to twenty minutes, it finally stopped and began to swim around in its own half of the aquarium.

When the barrier was lifted, the pike swam into the area from which it had been separated, but even though it was hungry and had been trying to get at the minnows only a few minutes earlier, it swam around them, never eating or so much as attacking one.

This famous experiment shows the prevalence of learned helplessness. It shows why most of us fail recognize those invisible barriers that keep us from achieving the things we want. The information in this book can help you eliminate the barriers around you. It can help you eradicate the fears that keep you from becoming successful.

## Three Techniques for Overcoming Fear of Success

Here are three techniques to help you overcome your fear of success. Because it primarily entails feelings of guilt, to overcome it we must convince ourselves that we deserve to have wonderful achievements—that we deserve success.

We all have developed conflicting ideas in our minds about how we should act and how successful we should be. Until we change these ideas and make it OK to succeed, we will continue to sabotage our own efforts. Try these three things:

1. List ten reasons why you deserve to make more than $200,000 a year, drive a new Porsche, or buy a new house.

2. Write down three things you may be doing to avoid achievement. These might include procrastinating, poor planning, having no

personal or business goals, or even refusing to implement new techniques and ideas. It's important to write these things down. You may also want to discuss them with your spouse or a friend in order to uncover possible success-sabotaging behaviors.

3. At the end of the day, write down at least one accomplishment of the day. In the evening, reward yourself for that success by eating your favorite dessert, watching your favorite television program, or reading your favorite book or magazine.

A financial consultant in Michigan who suffers from fear of success used similar techniques for eight weeks. His annualized income went from $50,000 to $150,000 during those weeks. At the end of the year, he bought a new Mercedes and is enjoying every day of it.

While other methods may be useful, these three techniques will certainly give you a good starting point for dealing with your fear of success.

Not everyone fears success. We all have a basic desire to be successful, and we live in a success-obsessed society. But you may fear success if during your childhood you experienced lack of parental approval, sibling rivalry, negative criticism, or conflicting messages.

If we have any of these fears—fear of rejection, fear of embarrassment, fear of failure, fear of success—it does not indicate that we're not right for the business we're in. It only means that we have self-sabotaging behaviors that keep us from reaching and maintaining the productivity level we need.

In nearly every case, when businesspeople are able to eliminate these fears, they make quantum leaps in their productivity and in their income.

The rest of this book is dedicated to helping you eliminate your fears, and, more importantly, giving you a design, an approach, and some techniques to help you have anything you could possibly want. If you can lay a game plan for realistic goals and you follow the Peak Performance Program laid out here, you can achieve your goals. You'll also be able to substantially increase your income within a short period of time. If you deal with your fears, manage the stress that occurs when you have them, and find the motivation to achieve, you will learn how to go from where you are to where you want to go.

# Seven

# What Self-Sabotaging Fears Can Do to Your Sales Performance

Self-sabotaging fears work hard to stop us from performing at peak production levels. In fact, sales management experts have found the biggest block to productivity is not our skill level or what we know about sales. It is more likely how much time we spend sabotaging our own production.

How much business could you handle if you stopped blocking your productivity with self-sabotaging fears? How much time do you waste reorganizing your desk or prioritizing phone calls or sitting in your chair thinking about what you are about to say to someone? How much anxiety do you feel in getting your confidence up to do battle in sales?

Too many people let their anxiety stump them. They sit at their chair looking at the telephone or rationalizing their way out of working effectively. It might be difficult to make excuses to the sales manager, but compared to the anxiety some people face about prospecting for new business, it's relatively easy. A salesperson might say, "I really can't originate any more business this afternoon. I have to prepare for my appointment with a prospect tomorrow." Or "This is a bad time to call that lead. He's obviously busy."

Individuals with high levels of self-esteem tend to experience fewer self-sabotaging fears. Sales managers recruiting successful producers not only look for high self-esteem, but also for those who are hungry. They believe candidates who are financially well off may not have the same determination to produce.

Too much anxiety may be paralyzing and keep you from putting yourself in situations where you may be rejected. But hunger to achieve and succeed is probably helpful for getting salespeople out of their armchairs to prospect for new business.

## Self-Esteem

To understand how self-esteem works, think of the gold vault at Fort Knox. Gold is valuable as a hedge against currency inflation. When the United States economy was linked to the gold standard, the dollar was pegged to the value of gold. The more gold the government had, the more paper money it could produce. The less it had, the worse off its economy was.

This concept parallels how self-esteem—the gold in our mind—works.

In your mind, you set the value of your self-esteem. The more value you place on yourself, the more "gold" you deposit in your mind. Real gold is put into the Fort Knox vault on deposit. Gold can also be withdrawn, but only at the same value. So gold worth $1,000 an ounce when it is deposited can only be withdrawn at $1,000 an ounce.

If you continually think of yourself as having difficulty making phone calls, you are making deposits of very low worth into your mental vault. When the time comes to make withdrawals for performing tasks such as prospecting, you will withdraw skills to which you've attached a low value. In other words, the gold you withdraw from your mental vault has the same low value as it had when you deposited it.

Other people can influence the value of your mental gold with their compliments, strokes, and praises. But it's your own self-appraisals and self-esteem that will trigger the self-sabotaging fears that can keep you from achieving your maximum potential.

Individuals with high self-esteem and high self-worth place an extremely high value on their mental gold. It is as if they had trained a guard to stand in the doorway of their mental vault. This guard rejects gold that has little value attached to it (perhaps as a result of negativity, self-depredation, or harsh self-reproach) and only allows deposits that have a very high worth.

## Understanding Our Own Behavior

In his famous works on psychoanalysis, Sigmund Freud determined that human beings develop their basic personalities between the ages of two and seven years. The developmental psychologist Jean Piaget later substantiated that this is when the imprinting process—when children largely take on the characteristics of their parents—takes place. If the parents tend to be overweight during these years of the child's development, the child may also unconsciously gain weight as well. If parents smoke in the house when the child is young, the child will have a strong tendency to smoke in later life. Although many "experts" will tell you that people can change any time they want with enough motivation, it is not that simple. Basic behavior changes, like stopping smoking, can take an enormous amount of work. Psychological fears—of failure, rejection, success, or embarrassment—may be equally difficult to change.

Marriage counselors often agree that second marriages are rarely more successful or problem-free than first marriages. When a wife divorces a husband for reasons such as lack of affection, she may do her best to marry a male the next time who is affectionate. Nevertheless, the second marriage is never problem-free. There are only different problems. She needs to focus on the real issue—her own behavior—and only secondarily on the behavior of her spouse.

The same is true of self-sabotaging fears. Because of my own fear of embarrassment, I had an extremely hard time speaking in front of audiences. This is fairly difficult to understand, since I make a substantial part of my living by speaking professionally to more than 1,000 people every week. For two straight years, however, I had difficulty sleeping for even ten minutes the night before a presentation. My fear that the audience would dislike my message, or me, was extreme. Decades later, I am still speaking to audiences around the world. I have not had difficulty sleeping for twenty years now. I was able to deal with my fear simply by hitting my head against a brick wall and eventually knocking it down. But behaviors are difficult to change completely. Even though I learned to cope with my fear of audiences and public speaking, I've still not erased it totally.

Years ago, I was asked by the president of my church's Sunday school class to do a nine-week lecture series on parenting. I realized I would have to go back to psychological manuals and books on the subject to gain a better understanding of how parents should deal with their children to bring them up as happy, responsible, and ethical high achievers.

I spent two to three weeks preparing for my presentation. But the day I was to speak to a group of seventy in the Sunday school class was also the day I became reacquainted with my fear of speaking. The night before my presentation, I was scared to death. I went to bed at 10:30 p.m. but probably didn't get to sleep until almost 3 a.m. I wasn't worried about the content as much as I was about doing a good job in front of people who knew me—in many cases, very well. My self-sabotaging fear of embarrassment returned. I sat in the Sunday school class twenty minutes before I was introduced. I felt my hands become clammy and my heart pound like a bass drum. When I was introduced, I walked to the front and felt my voice quaking and quivering; I also knocked the speaker stand down within thirty seconds of starting my speech. Obviously I had not lost my fear. But after many years, I had learned to cope with it.

## Reasons for Sabotaging Yourself

You already know that fears often produce avoidance behaviors. As stated earlier, these are behaviors we engage in to keep from feeling the painful effects of fear and anxiety. For example, being perfectionistic is an avoidance behavior. If you spend an inordinate amount of time typing a letter or writing an article and as a result have no time to make phone calls or straighten out a problem with a staff person, you are using an avoidance behavior to avoid a self-sabotaging fear.

In their book, *Treat Your Ego in Four Hours*, Tom Ruske, MD, and Randolph Read, MD, state that everyone uses avoidance behaviors or escapes as tools for everyday life. They can include behaviors such as sleeping, drinking, eating, or even reading at inappropriate times. They do not indicate mental illness, but simply an inability to cope.

Ruske and Read also suggest that we sometimes sabotage ourselves to achieve an unconscious hidden goal. For example, people may not be overweight only because they like to eat. They may use their physical shape to avoid putting themselves in positions where they may feel discomfort. If you are overweight, you might not think you are good-looking. You won't have to spend much time searching through stores to spend money on expensive, trendy clothing. You can stay at home more often, because you are asked to go out less. You may have fewer friends, because in our society people tend to pay more attention to and engage in conversation with attractive people. You also might lose some self-respect and find it more advantageous to let other people take pity on you. The real benefit to being overweight, then, is protecting oneself from relationships that might be too uncomfortable.

Some psychotherapists believe that women overeat to avoid rejection from men. If they spend hours each week exercising, grooming themselves, shopping for clothes, and dieting, they are, in effect, pushing themselves to be more physically attractive and available to the opposite sex. After all their work, if men still don't reward them for their effort by asking them out or paying attention to them, women may feel even more deeply rejected than when they were overweight. Why not avoid rejection by simply gaining weight?

A salesperson may react similarly and think, why risk rejection on the telephone? Simply don't make the phone calls. Odd as it may seem, people who avoid making calls when it is part of their job may be doing so because of the benefits they receive. One benefit is not giving the person on the other end of the line a chance to speak harshly to you. That secretary might not give you a tough time on the telephone. She won't have the chance to screen you and decide whether she will let you talk to the decision maker.

Another benefit of lower productivity is spending less time in the office and more time at home. Or perhaps it is letting friends and acquaintances realize you're just like them: you don't have to face the problem of making more money than your friends. In addition, if you don't make a lot of money, friends and relatives may expect less from you. Relatives don't come by to ask for money. You won't have to spend time talking to CPAs and financial planners to shelter your income from taxes.

## Weighing the Benefits of Tackling Fears

Take some time now to list at least ten benefits for not doing something you think you are afraid of. Whether they involve fears of rejection, embarrassment, failure, or success, list ten reasons you could have for using an avoidance behavior to achieve an unconscious hidden goal.

An avoidance behavior I have used, for example, is avoiding a call to the meeting planner to commit to a speaking date. If I don't call the meeting planner, I won't have to lose sleep the night before the presentation. I won't experience anxiety thinking about it. My anxiety won't increase when my wife asks me what I am going to speak about in the program. I won't have to go to the library and spend four or five hours' research to tailor my topic to the group's needs. I won't have to vividly recall my sleepless nights. I won't be distracted from doing other activities because I'm preoccupied with the upcoming presentation. I won't have to face embarrassing questions after my presentation. I won't have to deal with the group if they don't like my presentation. I won't have to worry about making future presentations to the same group. I won't have to make future choices about whether or not I should stay in my current career.

By listing the benefits of using avoidance behaviors, I am putting a worth on those benefits. By doing this, I then can weigh them against the favorable benefits of calling a meeting planner.

Next I would like you to write down the benefits of doing something you might be afraid to do. For, example, if you shy away from marketing calls, make a list of the positive benefits you get from making the calls. The benefits I might get from calling that meeting planner to commit to a date might include the following:

- I'd make money from the speech.
- I'd be able to travel to a different part of the world.
- I'd get applause after my presentation.
- People would flock to the front of the room asking for autographed copies of my book afterward.
- I might receive more respect from my family.
- I'd feel a greater sense of self-worth.
- I could save the money to buy a nicer car.
- I could use the money to feed my family.
- I'd feel good about being able to provide for my family.
- I'd enjoy my work more.

Once you have written down the benefits of *not* doing an activity as well as the benefits of doing it, you should be able to weigh one against the other. Because you're basing the decision on knowledge of both sides of the issue, this method is a very cognitive approach to determining whether or not a behavior is worthwhile.

All activities have a plus and a minus side. We've all sat down at one time or another and listed the benefits versus the drawbacks of doing something. Maybe it was accepting a lucrative job offer with a less than stable startup company. Or maybe it was deciding whether or not to go back to school. To make intelligent decisions about something, we have to know the downside as well as the upside.

If you refuse to weigh your options, you are simply telling yourself you have no control over your own behavior. On the other hand, if you convince yourself that everything you do is in some way useful to you, you will be taking on more responsibility for your actions. You'll be able to make clear business and personal decisions.

If you decide not to make prospecting phone calls, at least you will be aware of the benefits you think you are receiving as a result. When I worked as a consultant for a major computer firm, I came across a producer selling network servers to large corporations. His name was Mel. I asked Mel one day, "When you look at ways to increase production, have you found anything about the job that motivates you?" Mel confided to me that money was not all that important to him. What he really wanted was a chance to move up in the company. When I began working with him to outline a game plan for getting to the top of his company, he stopped me abruptly. He said, "When I really think about it, I guess I really don't want my boss's job. My boss has no power, lots of problems, and too many conflicts in his career. I really don't want that."

Mel was actually avoiding the opportunity to increase his sales production to prevent the risk of not being promoted. He eased up on his productivity because he had perceived definite benefits from not achieving superstar sales production. If his sales rose too high, he would likely be promoted, get more money, and be pushed into a managerial position he didn't want. For Mel, the promotion and money did not outweigh the drawbacks of the managerial position.

Are you like Mel? Have you consciously or unconsciously decided that you do not want the rewards, and problems, that success brings? Are you artificially keeping your production low by avoiding phone calls, spending a lot of social time with associates in your office, coming to work late, leaving early, or not reading books that could help develop your sales skills? Is this an unconscious strategy you are using to achieve your own preset goal?

After you have weighed the cost of not changing against the benefits of changing, you can decide whether to go through what could be a painful process of reworking certain behaviors.

Just like Mel, you may realize that the action involved in changing is not so difficult, but the results are not what you want. In that case, you would simply stay where you are. On the other hand, if you find that the benefits far outweigh the drawbacks, then you must determine how you want to change.

## How Do You Want to Change?

Ask yourself the following questions:

- When do you want to change?
- What is prompting you to change?
- What specifically would you like to change?
- What avoidance behaviors might you be using to avoid changing?

Change involves effort and risk. But if you have enough desire to change, that effort won't seem as difficult and the risk won't seem as fearsome. Rarely do any of us map out the four steps above when we want to change behavior patterns, but if we really want to change, looking hard at our answers to these questions will make the process easier.

Bethany, a real-estate agent I worked with, wanted to change her behavior to make more money. She wanted to change within thirty days. She was tired of netting only a few hundred dollars per month over her expenses. She wanted to be able to knock on at least ten doors each day and ask people if they wanted to list their homes. She realized she was rationalizing that she was too busy showing houses or doing paperwork in her office to knock on prospects' doors. Once Bethany knew when she wanted to change, exactly what was prompting her to change, and the avoidance behavior she was using to sabotage herself, she was well-armed to make that change.

## Play Therapy

Sometimes people sabotage their productivity by taking themselves too seriously. They are paralyzed in making decisions because they put too much importance on the possible outcome of their decisions. Remember: the decisions you make on a daily basis will not substantially make or break your sales career. Your career is the coordination of weeks, months, and years of effort. The actions of only very few of us have as huge an impact as those of the president of the United States who, by doing something as innocuous as forgetting to shake the hand of a dignitary from another nation, could align that other nation with a competing power.

Play therapy is a means, not of making a game out of what we do, but of taking frequent fun breaks throughout the day. It is far more difficult to use avoidance behaviors or feel the stressful effect of our fears if we enjoy ourselves during the day.

I recently spoke to a salesperson who started every phone conversation by talking about something nice or humorous he heard in the secretary's voice who transferred him to the prospect. For example, "Mr. Kemper, I really enjoyed talking to your secretary.

On the telephone, she sounds like a cross between actress Jennifer Lawrence and Martha Raddatz," the ABC news correspondent.

Because of the relationship, prospects will typically laugh or at least feel that the ice has been broken a bit. When you use humor with prospects, some of the pressure disappears. You'll have less of a chance of rejection and a more receptive audience for your proposal. When you can have fun in your conversations with prospects, you greatly increase the chance that you will call another directly afterward.

You should not only make sales situations fun, but also try to give yourself play breaks. Play breaks help take some of the pressure off during stressful situations in which you might be using avoidance behaviors. In these cases, take a brief break. You might try to remember an amusing film you saw or an interesting radio commercial you've just heard on your company's internal music system. You might observe a bit of ridiculousness in the way a person walks through the hallway. Or you may, as I do, pick up a sheet of paper, walk to an associate's desk, and tell them your favorite joke.

Some people may see taking time out from making phone calls as being undisciplined. But if it relaxes you and as a result makes you more productive, play breaks are a great way to take the pressure off and enjoy your workday.

Play breaks don't require a particular methodology as much as an attitude of moderation. An essential element of effective play breaks is to have enough discipline to keep them short and to stop the break from itself becoming an avoidance behavior. Used in small amounts, sprinkling play breaks throughout your day is much like putting a pinch of salt on mashed potatoes. You can greatly enhance the enjoyment of your meal, or of your work.

## The Three-Minute Phobia Cure

One of the most interesting and provocative ways to deal with your sabotaging fears is what psychotherapists Richard Bandler and John Grinder call their *three-minute phobia cure*. Through a process called *neurolinguistic programming*, Bandler and Grinder have confounded traditional psychotherapists for years. They believe many with fears and phobias unconsciously allow their psychotherapists to lull them into months and even years of counseling. At a rate of over $100 an hour, this becomes very lucrative for the psychotherapist. But Bandler and Grinder believe that people with fears have simply not allowed themselves to dissociate from feelings of past experiences. For example, when they picture their feared activity, such as driving on the freeway, they also imagine the panic they once felt some years earlier. They avoid this panic by not driving on the freeway, or, in some cases, by not driving at all.

Bandler's and Grinder's phobia cure simply helps the sufferer associate with pleasant memories and dissociate from unpleasant memories. While this may sound very simple, the hard part is to do it often enough, with enough concentration, that your brain molds the new fearless habit. Then the mind automatically triggers only pleasant memories and forgets unpleasant ones. They report that the three-minute phobia cure is one of the quickest and most persuasive ways of changing people and their specific behaviors.

Here is how it works: If you have a fear of being in elevators, for example, imagine you're sitting in the middle of a movie theater. On the screen, you see a black-and-white photograph of yourself in the situation you experienced just before you had the initial phobic response or anxiety, standing outside the elevator.

The next step is to imagine yourself, not in the middle of the theater, but in the projection booth. Here you can watch yourself still sitting in the middle of the theater, watching yourself in a still photograph on the screen.

The next step is to turn the photograph into a black-and-white movie. Back in the middle of the theater, you watch this film of yourself outside the elevator, walking into the elevator, followed by the events up to the end of the unpleasant experience.

Bandler and Grinder suggest that when you get to the end of the movie, you stop again on a final frame in the film and then suddenly jump inside the picture and roll the movie backward. Everybody and everything in the movie walks backwards, runs backwards—totally in reverse. You are basically rewinding the film, except that you are in the film watching yourself moving backwards through the elevator. The only rule in running the movie backwards is you must imagine it in color and take only one to two seconds to do it.

In this phobia cure, you distance yourself from your own actions by imagining that you're watching yourself watch yourself on a screen in a black-and-white movie of the entire unpleasant experience. You then undo the experience by imagining yourself jumping inside the picture and then running it rapidly backwards in color.

In a way you are ridiculing your phobic anxiety response in the elevator by imagining the experience as a sort of slapstick sight gag. But this method may also give you some relief from anxiety. By the end of the cure, you imagine yourself in color rapidly reliving this event from its point of highest anxiety backward to the point of no anxiety. You're going very quickly from bad to good.

This cure could also work with telephone calls. If you have a horrible fear of calling people on the telephone, you could simply imagine yourself in the middle of the movie theater, seeing up on the screen a black-and-white photograph of yourself just before making a phone call, which gives you very high anxiety.

Then imagine yourself in the projection booth, watching yourself watch yourself staring at the telephone about to make a call. Then turn that snapshot into a black-and-white movie and watch the movie progress from you staring at the telephone to making the telephone call, having a conversation, feeling the anxiety, and eventually hanging up.

Then stop the movie and stare at it as if it were a slide photograph. See yourself jumping inside this slide, then run the movie backward, in color, at an extremely rapid rate. You are actually becoming disassociated from the anxiety of the phobic experience of making that telephone call.

This cure has been used with great success. Many people have absolutely no symptoms of the phobia after the treatment, as well as no symptoms for weeks and months afterward.

Bandler and Grinder report they have helped thousands of people overcome specific phobias, as well as saving them as much as $70,000 to $100,000 in psychotherapeutic costs.

This technique is both simple and exceptional. Try it the next time you feel any anxiety about making a telephone call, seeing somebody face-to-face, speaking in front of a group, or when you find that any of the sabotaging fears—rejection, embarrassment, failure, or success—rear their ugly heads. The risk is minimal; the benefits may be enormous.

# Eight
# How to Eliminate Your Performance Barriers

## Using SUDS to Wash Away Self-Sabotaging Fears

Performance problems stem from experiencing some, or all of the four self-sabotaging fears:

- Fear of rejection
- Fear of embarrassment
- Fear of failure
- Fear of success

We avoid achieving our maximum potential because of the anxiety these fears bring us.

In extreme cases, our fears overwhelm us. Like the person in the last chapter's example of the phobia cure," some people are deathly afraid of riding in elevators. They're frightened of being suspended in a box going up and down in a building. All they can envision is a wire breaking or a motor malfunctioning.

The real reason people feel upset when riding elevators is not that they dislike moving up and down rapidly. It is that they fear the anxiety or discomfort they associate with the experience. Yet if we don't learn to live with our own anxiety, we'll never reach our full potential—our maximum productivity level. We'll continue to avoid building our business. We won't prospect for new clients or ask for referrals. We will actually avoid success.

## The SUDS Scale

There are indicators that you are sabotaging your performance. They let us know when we're suffering from self-sabotaging fears and anxiety has taken over and limits our performance.

One such measurement is called the SUDS Scale. SUDS stands for *Subjective Unit of Discomfort Scale*. Figure 8.1 features the SUDS Scale complete with its different levels of discomfort.

Psychologist Joseph Wolpe originated the SUDS Scale. He found that the different levels of anxiety and comfort we experience can be assigned relative positions.

The SUDS Scale ranges from 0 to 100. To the bottom of the scale—at the 0 level—Wolpe assigned the state of total relaxation. In most cases sleep is at the 0 level.

When we feel drowsy—as if we're about to fall asleep—we're at about the 5 level. When we're awake, experiencing nearly total comfort, we're at 10. At the 10 level, we may be thinking about taking a break and relaxing or even taking a nap. At 15, we're doing activities that require little motivation, such as driving to our offices, filing papers, or reading a light book.

At 20 on the SUDS scale, motivation sets in. In fact the range in which we are likely to begin to feel motivated is between the 20 and 30 level. At this level, we probably would feel compelled to see people. We may begin to do productive activities, such as planning

FIGURE 8.1 Subjective Unit of Discomfort Scale SUDS

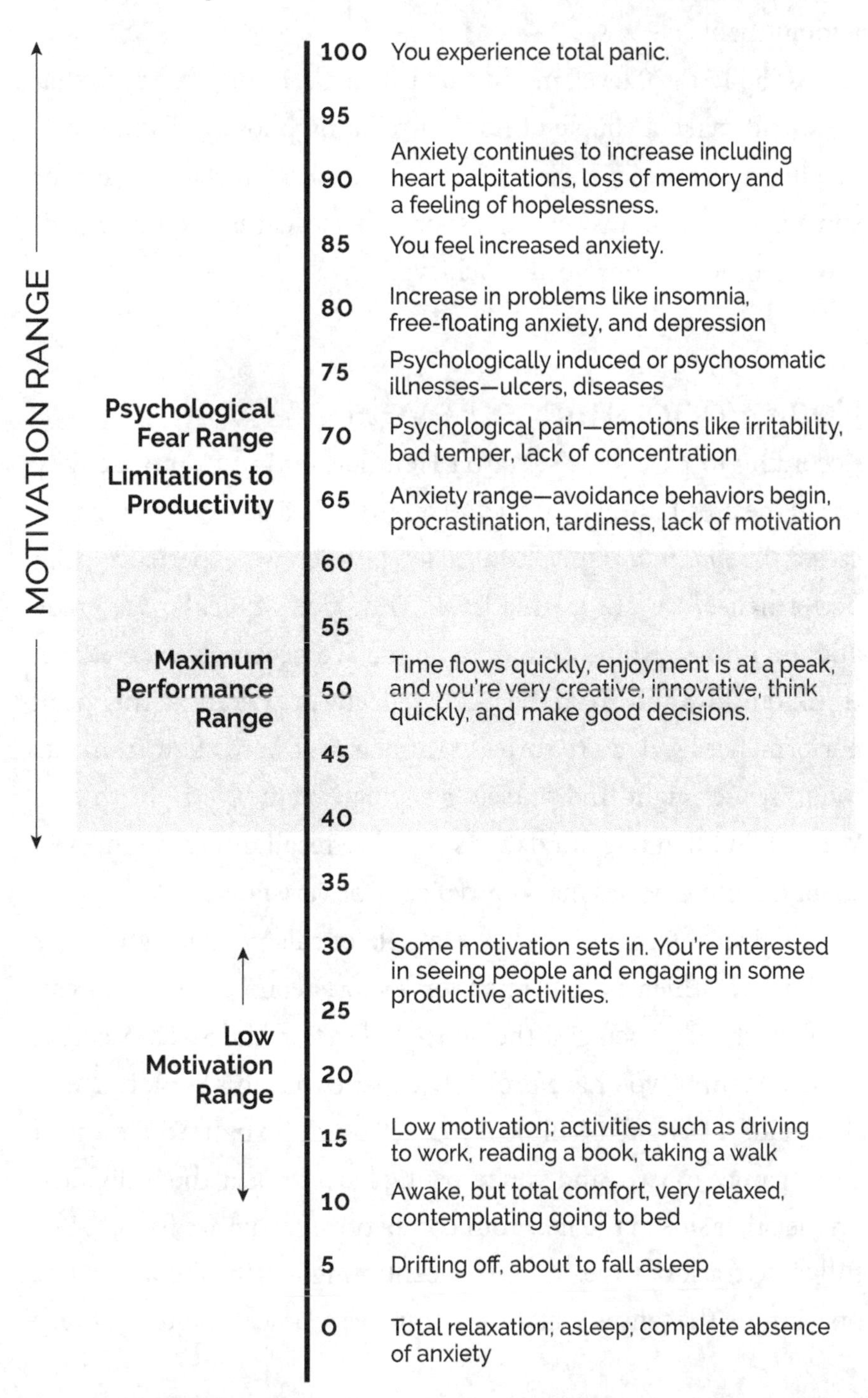

our day. Perhaps we'll work with our assistant to schedule some appointments.

At the 15 to 20 level, motivation isn't high. It might be such that we would make a couple of nonintimidating phone calls to someone like a business associate. We might even call a client to ask for some advice or to answer a question. This level may coincide with the beginnings of our need to achieve.

## Peak Performance Levels

According to psychologist Aaron Hemsley, optimum productivity lies in the area between 30 and 40 on the SUDS Scale. This range is called the *maximum performance level*. When we experience peak performance, we are at this level. Time flows quickly. We enjoy and are immersed in what we're doing. We become very creative, think quickly, and make decisions effectively. Often at this peak performance level, we're surprised at how well words flow from our mouths. We might find ourselves saying exactly the right things. We also find that our minds are sharp. We recall information, even though our memories may not typically be very good.

To give you an even better example of this peak performance level, when athletes are primed for a sports competition, you can think of them as being at the 30 to 40 level on the SUDS Scale. If you play tennis, you have probably experienced this peak range in the middle of a match. Think of yourself serving a ball. You're ahead three games to two, and you're trying hard to beat the individual on the other side of the net. Your competitive spirits are flaring. You fully lose track of time. You're concentrating totally and absolutely on winning the tennis match. You think very quickly. You react very fast. And you find that your concentration powers are probably at a height you've rarely experienced before.

The same thing may be true in golf. When you're playing, time goes by very quickly. You may even be surprised to realize that you've been out on the golf course for four hours. It really doesn't feel like it, because you're having such a good time.

If you've ever done any public speaking, you've probably felt the same sort of enthusiasm and excitement. After the first five or ten minutes, when your initial anxiety has gone away, your mind operates very quickly, and you become totally unaware of the time that you've spent speaking. (The audience could be aware of the hour, but you're having a great time.) Ideas flow quickly; you feel excited and enthusiastic. You really are at peak performance.

If we start feeling anxiety, we are up one level, to 45 on the scale. At this level, just above peak performance, we start experiencing avoidance behaviors. We may begin procrastinating. Perhaps we feel disorganized. We may even dread making phone calls.

At this level we would probably feel anxiety in asking for referral calls. We may even experience anger, become upset, or feel frustrated at trying to work on a problem or project.

If we experience more severe pain, we are at the 55 level. Psychologically induced, or psychosomatic, illness, such as tension headaches, migraines, or muscle pain or soreness, indicate the 60 level. We may be unable to concentrate or are easily distracted. We may find ourselves daydreaming. We also may become depressed or upset.

When we start to face severe problems, we are at the 70, 80, or 90 levels. We may become increasingly anxious, experiencing an almost phobic type of fear. Things begin to really bother us and give us deep psychological pain. We find ourselves bad-tempered and extremely irritable.

If you ever find yourself in total panic, you have reached the 100 level—the top of the SUDS Scale. Someone in one of my audiences described this 100 level as how you would feel if you're in your car "following a group of a hundred motorcycle-riding, chain-carrying Hell's Angels when your horn gets stuck."

Rarely do we ever experience such total panic. When we do, it might be in a situation like being stuck in a traffic jam when you have fifteen minutes to make a flight—the last flight of that day—for an extremely important meeting. Another example might be the experience the bank examiners had when they went in to close Lehman Brothers during the Great Recession and found that their baggage was lost, leaving them nothing more to wear during their stay than what they had on. Or reaching the 100 level on the SUDS may come from winning a trip to Mexico City in a sales contest, only to find out later that you have to win a trip back.

## Using Anxiety for Maximum Productivity

As we've seen, peak performance occurs between the 30 and 40 level on the SUDS. Even though we experience a small level of stress or anxiety, it works to our advantage. At this point discomfort or anxiety can actually help by motivating us. We might see our work as a challenge. We feel enthusiastic and excited about what we're doing. Time will flow very quickly and we'll be at peak performance. In this range we will be surprised at how much we can accomplish.

But if we have too much discomfort, say at level 60 or above, this will work against us and we'll actually sabotage ourselves.

When the fears we discussed—those of rejection, embarrassment, failure, or success—set in, we are at the 45 level or above on the SUDS. Our discomfort causes us to use avoidance behaviors, which keep us from doing activities that cause the painful anxiety.

The four fears I discussed, with their chief symptoms—anxiety and depression—only hurt us when they cause our SUDS level to rise to 45 or higher. If we can decrease our anxiety and discomfort, self-sabotaging fears will have no impact on our business or personal lives. We then can be as successful and as productive as we want to be, without limiting ourselves.

## Know Your SUDS Level

It's very important to be constantly aware of your SUDS level. In fact, you should check your position on it several times a day, using the scale in figure 8.1. It may be difficult to remind yourself to do this without using a memory jogger. Some good ways to jog your memory are things like placing a note that reads, "What Is Your SUDS?" on top of a paperweight. Another good memory jogger is to put something, say a rubber band, on the pen you usually write with. But one of the best methods I've ever heard is to use is clear fingernail polish. You could put a drop of it on the crystal of your watch. Fingernail polish won't stain the crystal, but will make an enamel finish on the crystal. Whenever you look at the time, you will be reminded to determine where you are on the SUDS Scale.

## Too Low to Motivate—Moving On Up

In a work situation, it is just as bad to be too low on the SUDS Scale as it is to be too high. If you are between 0 and 30, you probably don't have enough stress, or motivation, to bring yourself up to peak performance and peak productivity.

There are a number of good ways to move up on the scale to achieve maximum performance. One is to read motivational books and follow through on the methods they give. However, a common complaint about motivational books is that they're full of promise but not very effective—like sipping a teaspoon of water while you're walking across a hot desert. It tastes good, but it doesn't satisfy your thirst for long. Motivational books are very entertaining, but unfortunately their effect is short-lived.

Another way to move up the scale is to use chemicals. I'm talking about eating candy or drinking coffee or another drink with caffeine. Unfortunately, these are also bad, because consuming caffeine artificially stimulates the heart rate, and consuming sugar sharply increases blood-sugar levels. These substances give you a high for about half an hour to forty-five minutes. But when the effect wears off, you usually feel lower than you did before.

One of the best ways to move up the scale is to get your heartbeat level up by natural means. This helps the adrenaline system work for you instead of against you. When you get your heartbeat level up, you will feel that it has a similar effect to caffeine.

A great way to move up on the SUDS to the 30 to 40 level is to engage in a good physical exercise program. Activities like jumping rope, swimming, jogging, or even jumping on a trampoline will get your heartbeat level up and raise your SUDS level to peak productivity.

Unfortunately, it's sometimes difficult to go swimming or jogging in the middle of the day. That's why doing some minor exercise, like walking around your office, is a very good way to bring yourself up the scale. You should also do stretching exercises such as touching your tiptoes or twisting your waist. Some psychologists and doctors recommend that people get up one hour earlier in the morning and exercise. This not only gets us up the SUDS and gives us a sense of well-being, but it also starts us with a nice outlook on the day.

Getting up an hour earlier enables us to do things like play tennis or racketball. It's interesting to go to tennis or racketball courts at 6:30 or 7:00 in the morning and see how crowded they are. Apparently many businesspeople have already realized that if they get a rush of adrenaline through physical exercise in the morning, they will have a much better, more productive day.

If you tend to have a very productive morning but slow down around lunchtime, perhaps finding that your SUDS level decreases to about 10, you might consider doing some activity at noon. Instead of having a heavy lunch, perhaps you could eat a sandwich or an apple on your way to engage in midday recreation. Go play tennis or take a walk in a park. Do something as simple as walking down to a restaurant for lunch instead of driving.

## Self-Talk to Bring Up the SUDS

During the day, if you lose motivation and thus are slipping down the SUDS scale, one other technique works quite well to bring you back up: self-talk. One of the best things you can do for yourself is to affirm yourself. In fact, if you've ever driven alone on the highway late at night and you find yourself starting to fall asleep, one way that you can stay awake is to talk to yourself. Talking to yourself can increases your SUDS level. If you start talking back to yourself, you may be in for a psychological shock. But self-talk does often work very well to help us work out problems we may have internalized.

When we're able to hear our responses and our thoughts spoken out loud, they often sound a little ridiculous. Self-talking helps tune us back in to what's really important and what's real in life.

If you don't wish to hold conversations with yourself, perhaps you could give yourself self-motivational affirmations such as "I'm looking good," or "I'm going to be successful today." You've probably even heard some people reciting their favorite motto, such as "Today is the first day of the rest of my life," or "Every day in every way, I'm getting better and better, and this is going to be my best day ever."

## Moving down the Scale

You also need to know ways to move down the scale. If you're above a 45 level, you're destroying your productivity. Your anxiety is too high. You're causing yourself to dread your work. You may use avoidance behaviors like procrastination and disorganization, and you may avoid making necessary phone calls.

Anxiety may be controlling you at this stage. When you're anxious, your muscles become tense. It's a natural stress response. Too much adrenaline flows through your body; your muscles tense up, causing headaches. You may also become increasingly upset. But if you can get a friend or even an office mate to rub your shoulders for a moment, your tenseness will usually dissipate and you'll move down the SUDS while you're being massaged.

Probably the best way to move down the SUDS is by using progressive relaxation. The best time to start using this technique is in solitude in the evening. Do it by yourself in a quiet room in a very comfortable chair. Loosen your tie or unbutton your collar, and relax as much as you can. Imagine yourself going into a peaceful, wooded forest. Spend approximately five minutes imagining walking into the forest, about twenty minutes imagining yourself in the forest, and five minutes walking out.

Then do this exercise during the day whenever your SUDS level is higher than 45. Take about ninety seconds to two minutes. Have your assistant hold your calls. Take about three deep breaths and exhale slowly. Visualize yourself back in the forest for just about one minute, take three more breaths, and go back to work. This will drop you down to the peak performance level, making you more productive than perhaps you have been in years.

I worked with a securities broker recently who told me that he could usually predict when he was moving above the 45 level. He would start grabbing his pencils more tightly. In fact, he would often break them. He'd feel tense and frustrated much more easily when making phone calls, which would raise his SUDS level even higher. He'd also find himself dreading having to make those calls. I taught him the progressive relaxation technique so that every time he started feeling he was above the 45 level, he would sit back in his chair, even though he was in a room with ten other salespeople. He would close his eyes for ninety seconds and, after taking three deep breaths, would think of himself in that forest. When he opened his eyes again, he was at his peak productivity level—totally ready, willing, and able to make another call. He found rejection had much less effect on him. He experienced much less tension and was much more effective in his job.

Obviously, when we experience less anxiety doing activities that makes money for us, like making phone calls or talking to clients, we will become much more profitable. In fact, we'll be very surprised at how productive we'll be—and at the amount of money we will make.

# Nine

# Staying in Your Peak Performance Range

## How to Beat Call Reluctance

David prides himself on being thorough. He considers himself to be a pro, but he'd like his sales production to be a little higher. He's tired of watching new producers outperform him. They really don't know everything about their product. He, on the other hand, is always prepared and knows exactly what to say. The problem is, he doesn't say it often enough. Rather than face his fear of failure, he'd rather spend time analyzing than acting.

Brian considers himself successful. He is image-conscious and knows how to act appropriately. Prospects like to deal with people who have style and class. Brian wants to be nothing short of the very best salesperson around. His self-image affects his behavior. He doesn't prospect much because he feels it is beneath him. To avoid his fear of embarrassment and possible loss of self-perceived status, he dedicates much of his time to industry organizations and professional groups. He rationalizes that networking is better than prospecting. He would rather rely on word of mouth to get new clients. Unfortunately, relying on others to refer prospects to him has never paid off. Brian figures it's at least better than exposure to prospects who don't know him.

Patricia enjoys selling. She likes helping people solve their problems. But she realizes that selling, while extremely profitable, can also be uncomfortable. She doesn't like to prospect on referrals or cold calls. She is afraid of being thought of as pushy and intrusive. She frequently apologizes to prospects for interrupting them. She hesitates to pick up the phone and start dialing, waiting for the right time to call. Patricia realizes she doesn't make a lot of calls, but she is unwilling to deal with her fear of rejection and take the risk of appearing too forward.

## Identifying Call Reluctance

These people's self-sabotaging fears have resulted in call reluctance. Do you identify with any of them? If you realize your productivity is low or that you are prospecting at low levels, you could have call reluctance. You have goals and the motivation to achieve these goals, but you find it emotionally difficult to get yourself to prospect and thereby to achieve those goals. According to *The Psychology of Call Reluctance* by George L. Dudley and Shannon Goodson, more than 40 percent of salespeople have experienced call reluctance to such a degree that it nearly ended their careers.

Most managers recognize that call reluctance is the main reason new salespeople fail, but few comprehend the impact it can have on more experienced producers, causing them to become complacent about prospecting calls.

A financial planner who has been in business for more than ten years wrote me recently. I am on friendly terms with him, since we see each other every week at our church Sunday-school class. He knows me well enough to call by phone, but instead he sent me a four-page boilerplate prospecting letter. It must have taken him at least an hour to dictate, not to mention the time his secretary took to type it. The letter described his company's background as well as his recommendations concerning my personal finances. It was so impersonal that I erased my name, scratched in "Dear Occupant," and showed it to my wife. She thought it was a joke, and we promptly tossed it into the trash. A standard, impersonal letter may work as a cold entry, but it indicated that my friend was experiencing call reluctance by not picking up the phone and calling me.

## Types of Call Reluctance

The first step in dealing with call reluctance is to recognize what it is and how it is affecting you. While there are numerous character types who experience call reluctance, four stand out as the most common:

- Analyzing reluctant
- Image-conscious
- Position accepting
- Fearful of intrusion

### THE ANALYZING RELUCTANT

Analytic call reluctance occurs in salespeople who are overly concerned about being swept away by their emotions. Afraid to show their true feelings, they preoccupy themselves with highly technical matters. Analytics keep their feelings in the deep freeze. They are afraid to reveal themselves because they suffer from the fear of rejection. They overanalyze and underact, appearing reserved and self-restrained in interpersonal conversations. When they give sales presentations, they tend to stress information while neglecting emotions. They sometimes even seem cynical about the value of interpersonal relations and people skills.

When I was a stockbroker, I knew an analytic type named Frank. He had been with the firm for about five years and was very knowledgeable. In between my daily load of 150-plus cold calls, I would pop into his office for inspiration and advice. Each time I saw Frank, he was looking over a stock's performance history or working on one of his stock algorithms. I was shocked to learn that out of the fifteen or so producers in our company, he was in the bottom 25 percent.

## THE IMAGE-CONSCIOUS TYPE

The image-conscious type of call reluctance is prevalent in salespeople who try to overcome self-confidence and self-esteem insecurities by making a show of the trappings of success. These people commonly suffer from fear of failure and often fear of success as well. They invest heavily in the appearance of wealth and achievement.

Ostentatious in their displays of success, this type maintains a constant vigilance against any threat to their advertised respect and net worth. In an effort to impress others, they often work on showy if not difficult cases. Lacking qualifications or experience, they nevertheless spend time working on big endeavors with a low probability of success, believing these infrequent "hot" deals are compatible with their perceived professional image. Sales in general is beneath them and is seen as just plain undignified.

An insurance agent I know fits this mold. He wears so much gold jewelry that he looks like an executive Mr. T. He often employs others to make cold calls because of what he says is his lack of time.

His production is low because he is still "streamlining his operation." He has a condescending way of speaking softly that makes others uncomfortable. You get the feeling that he sells a few large cases per year (which he brags about), although his profit margin is barely enough to support his financial needs. He continues to avoid prospecting until he's financially forced back into it to create more business.

## THE POSITION-ACCEPTANCE TYPE

The position-acceptance type of call reluctance occurs when salespeople suffer from fear of embarrassment. They are embarrassed or apologetic in their role as salesperson. They often suppress their sense of dedication and zeal because they don't believe their job or position is professionally impressive. They sense they are a disappointment to some significant person in their lives. Position-acceptance types may suffer from periods of job-related depression. While pretending to be committed, they never fully believe the job will become a career. They may not believe that sales, or at least the type of sales they do, is valid or worthwhile.

I speak frequently to insurance organizations populated by CPAs, CFPs, MBAs, or others who feel sales is not a career for those with smarts. Recently a new insurance agent showed me his card. Linked with a major life-insurance company, he had been in the field only about eighteen months. Instead of saying "Insurance Agent," the card introduced him as "Leigh Smith, Financial Consultant." I asked him if he sold securities. He said, "Not really. I actually sell insurance products." He probably had no idea that he was exhibiting classic signs of suffering from the position-acceptance type of call reluctance.

## THE FEAR-OF-INTRUSION TYPE

Fear-of-intrusion types don't want to be considered pushy or too aggressive. They frequently suffer from fear of embarrassment. Fear-of-intrusion types are unwilling to be assertive in prospecting for new business. They frequently lose control of the conversation or appointment, demonstrating an unwillingness to keep the prospect focused on the purpose of their call—that is, when they do actually prospect. They are overly concerned about the needs and desires of other people. A fear-of-intrusion type may postpone making a prospecting call because he or she is waiting for the right time to call or for an assurance that the prospect really wants to talk with him or her. Unfortunately, the salesperson is rarely able to find this "right" time, "right" person, and "right" place. Fear-of-intrusion types might make a call on a qualified referral but are very reluctant to call on prospects.

These people frequently accept a prospect's objections too quickly and have trouble closing a sale. They may view highly aggressive salespeople as unprofessional. While they are warm and sociable, they often let the needs of others take precedence over their own objectives.

I spent a few hours with a new salesperson, observing her prospecting skills. She was excited about dealing with people on the telephone but was a little intimidated by gruff prospects. I listened to her approach. She said, "Hi, Mr. Prospect. My name is Alana Berg. I'm with Prime Investment Company. Did I interrupt anything? Were you busy? If so, I could call back later." That's all 1 needed to hear. I quickly zeroed in on her lack of assertiveness. She said she had trouble believing that what she wanted to talk about was as important as what the prospect was doing when she called. She clearly suffered from the fear-of-intrusion type of call reluctance.

## Dealing with Call Reluctance

Albert Ellis PhD, a leader in Rational Emotive Therapy, has an interesting way of dealing with phobics. He believes that we engage in a series of irrational thoughts to support a fear—whether it is a fear of heights, a fear of asking a prospect to buy a product or service, or any of the four self-sabotaging fears that limit our productivity. These irrational mental processes reinforce our own negative self-image. For example, a salesperson might pick up a telephone and internally worry, "This prospect really isn't a very good referral. I've dealt with this type of person before. They're rude and curt. I really don't think now is a good time to call. Executives like this always get lots of calls in the morning from salespeople. I think I'll wait until the afternoon when things slow down for him."

Ellis believes that if we can interrupt and replace such internal dialogues with irrational thought patterns, we can allow ourselves to lose this extra baggage we carry.

## Four Easy Steps to Getting Rid of Call Reluctance

Use these four steps the next time you have a bout of call reluctance:

- Observe
- Pattern-interrupt
- Substitute
- Reward

### OBSERVE

First, observe yourself experiencing call reluctance. Pay careful attention to what you are going through. Chances are you have let your self-sabotaging irrational thoughts drag your personal esteem through the mud. As you did with Bandler's and Grinder's three-minute phobia cure in chapter 7, try detaching yourself from your thoughts and behavior. Be an observer instead of a participant.

An insurance agent recently tested this method. Just as he was about to make a call to a referral lead, he started feeling call-reluctance panic. His palms became moist and his heart palpitated. He also became aware of his irrational mental dialogue: "I really don't want to make this call. I feel myself becoming afraid of the telephone. If the prospect thinks I am intruding on his time, what will I say? He won't think I warrant any of his time because he'll know I'm new at this type of call. He'll probably recognize how scared I am of talking with him." The agent observed how his fears were influencing his thought.

## PATTERN-INTERRUPT

The second step is to interrupt the destructive behavior pattern. When we recognize when the irrational thought patterns of call reluctance are setting in, we can interrupt ourselves. Irrational thoughts seem to feed on themselves in a compounding way, like a snowball increasing in size rolling down a snowy hill.

Next time you observe that call-reluctance patterns have surfaced, immediately do something physical. Stand up and walk around your office. Say out loud what you are thinking.

One of the best ways to interrupt the pattern is to cause quick physical discomfort. Wear a rubber band around your wrist, and when you become self-sabotaging, snap the band. The sting will break the cycle.

## SUBSTITUTE

Third, immediately substitute a positive experience to replace a negative one. If you have been selling for even a few weeks, you have probably made a successful phone call. Recall how easy that call was and how good you felt during and after the conversation. Get a 3 x 5 file card, write down that name, and record every detail of how you felt during and after that call.

## REWARD

Finally, after every call, give yourself an immediate reward. Whether you were able to speak to your prospect or not, reward yourself. A reward can be anything from a sip of coffee to calling your spouse—or even popping a breath mint into your mouth. The reward reinforces the call and increases the likelihood that you will make another one.

A financial planner with the fear of intrusion recently used this four-step technique. He realized that he felt almost apologetic for even making a phone call. His heart palpitated and sweat beaded on his forehead before his calls. Then he observed his own phobic reaction, interrupted himself with a rubber-band snap, substituted it with a memory of a successful call, and drank a cup of coffee as a reward after he made the call. Not only did his level of anxiety decrease, but he finally was able to increase his revenues on the telephone and also to call past referrals for appointments he had put off for months.

If you are good on the phone, you'll be light-years ahead of your competition. Your productivity will increase. When you can learn to recognize how the four self-sabotaging fears can cause call reluctance, and you can identify the type of call reluctance you have, then you can do something about it. When you do, business will simply flow to you.

# PART TWO

# DESIGNING YOUR OWN PERFORMANCE PROGRAM

# Ten

# Setting Objectives

## The Hands-on Tools

You now have information that will enable you to recognize the psychological barriers to better performance. You can monitor your level of psychological discomfort and overcome anxiety. Now you can begin to build a tailor-made performance program for achieving your objectives.

### Deciding What You Want

First, we begin with goals and goal-setting. A goal is defined as the *terminal point of a race*. This is really the focus of this book—to help you accomplish your race toward a goal, whether it is to lose weight, modify your child's behavior, own your dream car or house, or make your company the most profitable ever in its industry. We want you to get your goals.

Consider goals other people have set. (If you have already set your own goals, don't tune out. The theory and methodology may help you refine your already set goals into more workable ones.)

Relax. We are not going to go into great detail about why you need to have goals or how to set them. In fact, we assume you have already set at least one or several goals and are looking for a way to achieve them. If you haven't, you can easily come up with something you would like to have. Think of something you've always wanted.

To build your tailor-made performance program, it is crucial to have some basis for your goals as the first step in this goal-getting system. Years ago, a friend of mine named Ty Boyd, a talk-show host on a local television station in North Carolina, was busy looking for people to interview. He found out that H. L. Hunt, the billionaire who with only a fifth-grade education had made his fortunes in oil and ketchup, was going to be in the North Carolina area. Boyd promptly sent a letter to Hunt asking if he would be on the show. Hunt replied that he would love to, but because of his schedule, he could not do it for six months.

The time went by very slowly as Ty kept thinking about Hunt, the man who won his first oil well in a game of five-card stud. Hunt swapped the well for oil leases and then struck a hard bargain with a legendary wildcatter named Columbus "Dad" Joiner. Hunt then gained control of a vast oil field in East Texas. At one point it was rumored that Hunt had personally earned $1 million in one week—and that was in 1943!

Finally, Hunt appeared on the program. After fifteen to twenty minutes of chatting with Hunt about the economy and his favorite investments, Boyd asked him a question he had been waiting months to ask. He asked, "How did you become so successful so fast?"

As Hunt paused for the answer, Ty remembered concentrating so hard on what Hunt was about to say that he forgot about the studio audience—all he could think about was the information that would change his life totally. But the reply was startlingly obvious.

Hunt said simply, "Decide what you want." That was all Hunt said. Simple? But this thought helped him become as wealthy as anyone could be in this country. Hunt went on to add one other thing, however: "Decide what you want, but also decide what you'll do to get it."

It's easy to desire things. But are we really prepared to make the sacrifice, to work hard for what we want? There are no magical pathways, no fast freeways. We must make a decision about what we really want; otherwise we'll flounder like a ship with no rudder. A friend of mine once observed that most people are waiting for their ship to come in, but unfortunately they're waiting at the bus depot.

## Know What Race You're Running

Unless you want to drift through life, undirected like a helium-filled balloon set free, you must set goals. Set objectives; otherwise you'll never know exactly what you're working toward or what race you're running.

Look at figures 10.1 through 10.4, all titled "Objectives." Study figures 10.1–10.3, then, using the blank objective sheet in figure 10.4 as a model, please write, in the spaces provided, the goals you want to achieve in the next one, three, and five years. Make sure these are goals you truly want—goals you are willing to work for.

FIGURE 10.1 Objectives

| OBJECTIVES | COST | WHEN |
|---|---|---|
| 1. Porsche Cayenne S | $110,000 | December |
| 2. Vacation in Europe | $15,000 | June |
| 3. Rental property | $400,000 | March |
| 4. Top Producer Award | $150,000 | December |

The goals you list should be specific and tangible. They must be achievements for which you can chart a plan. They should also be measurable. Goals such as "being happy" are important and nice but are not specific enough for this sales-performance program.

The objective "to make more money" is not specific at all. If you want to make $250,000 more per year, that is specific. If you want to write, "I want to be happy," then specify exactly what would make you happy. If doing business in a new market would make you happier, then write in a specific target number of sales you want to achieve in that market. If starting a new company would make you happier, write that in too.

Specify exactly what you want in the next one, three, and five years. These are your short-, medium-, and long-term goals.

FIGURE 10.2 Objectives

| OBJECTIVES | COST | WHEN |
| --- | --- | --- |
| 1. Read 1 book per week | 30 minutes per night | Within 30 days |
| 3. | | |
| 5. | | |

**HOW ATTAINED**

By using reward system and reading for 30 minutes every evening, so my level of reading activity slowly goes up to 1 book per week.

FIGURE 10.3 Objectives

| OBJECTIVES | COST | WHEN |
| --- | --- | --- |
| 1. Control child's messiness | 30 minutes per day | In 30 days |
| 3. | | |
| 5. | | |

**HOW ATTAINED**

By rewarding child's neatness and staying on contract until end of program. Also, this will be attained by abiding the terms of the contract.

FIGURE 10.4 Objectives

| OBJECTIVES | COST | WHEN |
| --- | --- | --- |
| 1. | | |
| 3. | | |
| 5. | | |
| HOW ATTAINED | | |

There are two basic types of goals: business or financial goals and personal goals (that is, what do you want for your family or for yourself in the next one, three, and five years?) Be sure to include both types of goals on your objectives list. When you have completed your list, place it in a spiral notebook or a folder. Use this as your Peak Performance workbook.

## Visualize Your Goals

The second step in building your goal-setting productivity program is *visualizing your goals*. Remember how when we were children we all used pictures to reinforce our goals or the things we wanted to achieve? In fact, young children or teenagers often put on their bedroom walls posters or photos of people they look up to, such as Superman, Wonder Woman, Iron Man, and even the Hulk. Later on, pictures of music and rock stars or sports heroes find their place on children's walls.

As adults, we can use the same technique to accomplish and achieve the objectives we want. Usually we try to remember goals in our minds. They are quickly forgotten however, because we don't have physical reminders, like those posters of heroes, to remind us of what we want.

We need to do the same thing we did when we were children: put a picture or a poster up in your office or on the bathroom mirror. An equally good method is to use a picture or an advertisement from a magazine that depicts exactly what we want.

We may think that we are more sophisticated than children; we don't need to use a child's tricks to remind us of what we want.

Let's look at an inspirational winner from the sports world from whom we can learn a lot about goals and see how he used this "child's trick" to become the "World's Greatest Athlete."

Most people remember that in the 1976 Olympics, Bruce (now Caitlyn) Jenner won a gold medal for the decathlon. He defeated both the Russian and East German star decathletes. But most people do not recall that in 1972, Bruce Jenner was also in the Olympics, in Munich. In Munich, Jenner placed tenth in the decathlon. Heartbroken, he decided he would do something to improve his performance and also keep his ambition and motivation at a peak.

In 1972, Jenner saw a newspaper article depicting that year's Olympic winners. The article heralded the greatness of the 1972 decathlon winner, Russian Nikolai Avilov, who had scored more points in the decathlon than any previous decathlete. Jenner cut the article out of the newspaper and put his own picture over the photo of Avilov. He also wrote in the distances and race times that he wanted to achieve in each event in 1976, when he was determined to go back to the Olympics and try again for the decathlon gold medal. In his California apartment, Jenner put the newspaper clipping with his picture, the distances, and the race times on his bathroom mirror so that he would look at it every day. He knew that if he committed it to memory by seeing it every day, he would achieve his goal four years later. Jenner not only was able to achieve his goal of winning the decathlon gold medal, but he also was able to surpass every distance and time that he visualized. He surpassed all expectations, scoring a greater number of points than anyone before in the Olympic decathlon event.

Every day he had been reminded by the picture to visually reinforce himself and give himself a motivational charge.

Look at figures 10.5 and 10.6, titled "Visualized Objectives." Look at figure 10.5 to see how someone used the visualized objective sheet to get a new BMW 650i Convertible.

To your own visualized objective sheet, attach a photo or a magazine clipping showing the objects you want to try to get within the next one, three, and five years. Put that photo or clipping in the space provided. Below it write down what it is, how much it costs, when you want it, and what you'll have to do to get it.

Put a copy of the visualized objective sheet you've created on the front of the folder or notebook you are using as your productivity workbook so that every time you look at the workbook, you'll have to look at the pictures of the things you want to achieve. This will help improve your overall attitude about working hard to get the things you want. It will also help you to keep clearly in mind exactly what you're working for.

FIGURE 10.5 Visualized Objective

| OBJECTIVES | COST | WHEN |
|---|---|---|
| 1. BMW 650i convertible | $99,000 | December |

**WHAT WILL YOU DO TO GET IT?**
Sell 2 products per week at average commission of $4,100 each.

FIGURE 10.6 Visualized Objective

(PLACE PHOTO HERE)

| OBJECTIVES | COST | WHEN |
| --- | --- | --- |
| 1. | | |
| 2. | | |
| 3. | | |
| 4. | | |
| 5. | | |

**WHAT WILL YOU DO TO GET IT?**

# Eleven
# Game Planning

## Applying the Goal to Averages

Goals are tremendous, but they mean absolutely nothing if we don't know how hard we have to work to get them. It's like starting a race without knowing the course, the distance to be covered, or the time or speed expectations.

To achieve any goal, we first need to know about how much effort we need to expend to reach that goal. Most people set a goal without understanding what they have to do to get it. All too often, they aren't prepared for the effort or cost they must expend.

Anyone can have a goal. Few people achieve their goals, however, unless they know specifically what they want and how hard they are willing to work to get it. Based on the information in this chapter, you can design a basic plan which can help you plot out exactly how much work you will have to do to achieve whatever objective you have in mind.

## The Three-Point Basic Objective-Setting Plan

1. **Figure the cost.** Figure out first how much your goal will costs in terms of dollars, time, or, in the case of weight loss, pounds. If your objective is a five-bedroom house, how much does it cost? What are you willing to put down as a deposit and how large a mortgage payment are you willing to make?

   If you want to lose weight and feel that membership in a health spa or gym is necessary, write down the cost. You should also decide how much time every day you are willing to spend exercising at the spa.

2. **Decide when you want to reach your goal.** Specify the year and even the month as closely as possible. When do you want your dream house? "As soon as possible" is too vague. Mark down a month. What month are you prepared to successfully end your diet? Or what month do you want to complete that fence you've been thinking about?

3. **Determine what you need to do.** You know it's probably not filing paperwork that would help you reach that objective. More likely, it's selling more products. Decide exactly what you need to do to achieve your goal by the date you want it. What activity will help give you your objective? Prospecting in a new market? Or just plain seeing more clients? If your objective is being more efficient in the morning, your activity might be getting to work a half hour earlier. Or writing a "things to do" list during the first fifteen minutes you're in your office.

**The Three-Point Basic Objective Setting Plan**

1. Figure the cost.
2. Decide when you want your goal.
3. Decide what you must do.

If you use it right away, it will help you become organized in setting up your sales-performance program. It will help you reach your objectives. Now you have set your goal, and you know how much it costs, exactly when you want it, and what activities you need to do to get it. For example, if your objective is a 550 SL Mercedes, how many more sales per month do you need to make to acquire that car when you want it? How many more face-to-face appointments must you go on during the month to make the additional sales? How many more appointments must you book during the day, week, and month to achieve that goal? How many more phone calls must you make during the day, week, and month?

## Chart Your Current Activity

To get an idea of how hard you are currently working, refer to figure 11.1, "What Are Your Averages?" and figure 11.2, "Current Activity" on the next page. Use figure 11.1 to figure out how many booked appointments and sales calls you actually make to get one sale. For example, one sale for you may require forty calls, which result in four booked appointments, or three actual appointments (since some appointments are inevitably canceled). If you get an $800 commission for each sale, then one call would be worth $20 to you.

FIGURE 11.1 What Are Your Averages?

1 sale = # appointments = # booked appointments = # calls
(For example: 1 sale = 3 appointments = 4 booked appointments = 40 calls)
If 1 sale = $800 commission, then 1 call = $20

Using figure 11.2, you can determine whether or not your current activity is helping you achieve your goal. These figures can be used for sales behaviors or any other target behaviors you would like to reach.

FIGURE 11.2 Current Activity

What are you currently doing each day and week to reach your goal?
# sales/week or day = # appointments/week or day =
# booked appointments/week or day = # calls/week or day

Other Target Behaviors

Tardiness: How often are you late (or on time)?
Reading: How many pages are you currently reading each day/week?
How often does your child misbehave?
How often does your child follow instructions?
How many pounds do you want to lose?

Use figures 11.3 to 11.5 as models for charting your current activity. If your target behavior is to make more sales, your graph may look like figure 11.3, where phone calls equal a straight line, booked appointments a broken line, and sales a dotted line. Figure 11.4 shows a similar graph with reading as the target behavior. Figure 11.5 (page 130) charts a child's good behavior as the target.

FIGURE 11.3 Activity Graph for Sales

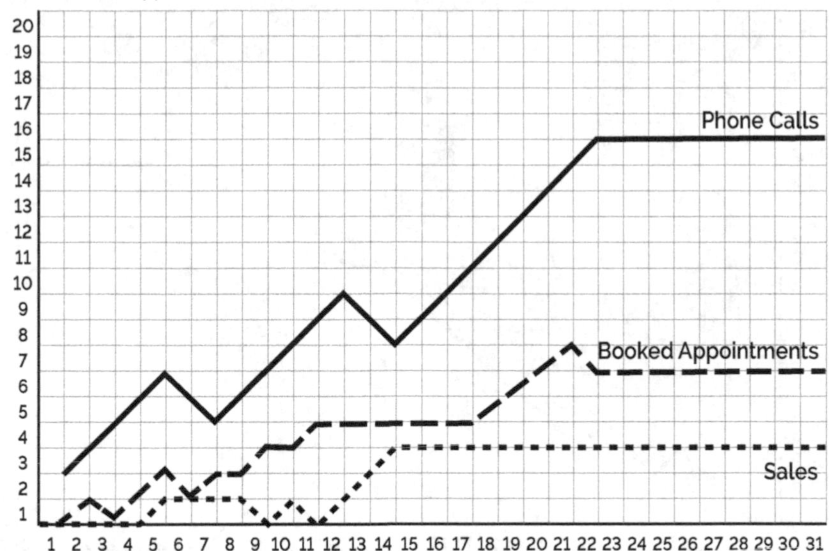


FIGURE 11.4 Activity Graph: Reading

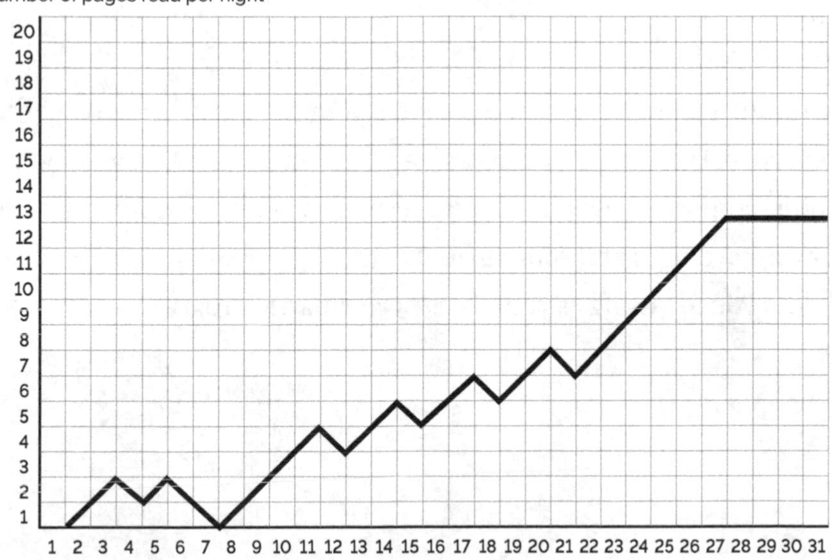

FIGURE 11.5 Incidences of Good Behavior

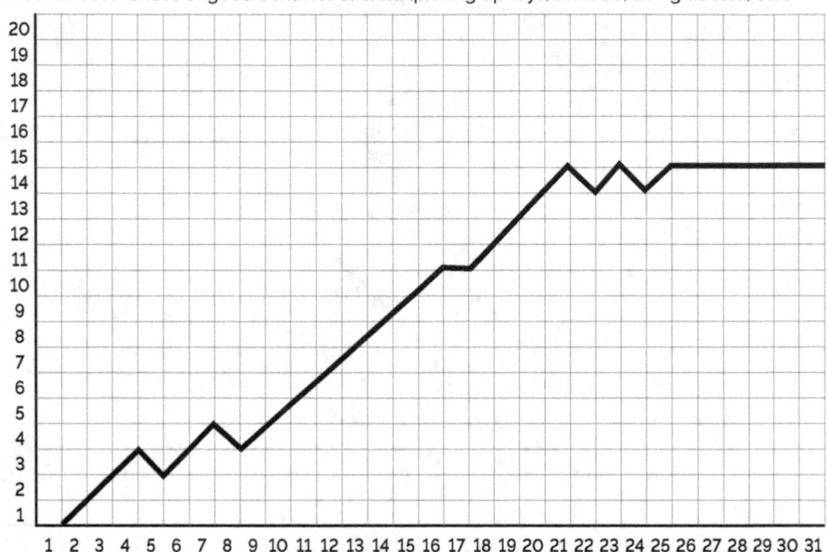


## Current Activity Graph

### GAME PLANNING: APPLYING THE GOAL TO AVERAGES

Working through how you'll perform your activity when you set the objective will give you a good idea of how hard you'll have to work for it, compared to your current level of productivity. Keep a copy of your averages and your current activity graph in the notebook or folder you are using as your sales performance program workbook.

# Twelve
# Building Your Averages

## Your Immediate and Deferred Reward Systems

One of the only ways we can achieve a goal is to know our habit patterns and performance averages—or our present modus operandi. When we have a handle on how we spend our time and how much effort we are expending, we may be very surprised.

### Knowing Your Averages

Many of us fall into ruts. Day after day, we start to fall into habits of doing things that are very nonproductive. We take on behaviors that cause us to avoid activities we need to do—activities that would help us perform more efficiently and effectively.

You should ask yourself the following questions once a month, if not once a week, because knowing your current activity-level and production averages (see figures 11.1 and 11.2, page 128) is essential to being productive:

- What are your current levels of activity?
- How much are you doing right now to get what we want?

- How much work are you doing to get our job done?
- What are you doing right now to make more money?

Or ask these questions:

- What are you doing now to lose that weight?
- What methods are you using to discipline your children?
- What are you doing right now to achieve your goals?

You can never hope to succeed unless you know exactly how you spend your time. I recently talked to a very depressed new salesperson, who hated to call prospects. After interviewing him for a few hours, I finally found out how he was spending his time and what his averages were. I found that his averages were very poor: out of every twenty calls he made, he would only get one appointment. Normally for his type of business, it took ten calls to get an appointment. But even though his averages were poor, he discovered that for each phone call, based on the commission he was receiving, he made roughly $30. In other words, for every twenty calls he made he would schedule an appointment, which down the line would give him one sale, so that for every twenty calls he was making approximately $600.

Think of how much more motivating it is to make those calls knowing each one yields $30. Instead of viewing the nonproductive calls as rejections or as worthless, each call—results or not—is worthwhile. If you're in sales or management, you probably already know that if you put in a high degree of effort and activity you will profit from your labors. You reap what you sow.

In this example, if the salesman wanted to increase his income by $20 each day, he would have to make seven additional phone calls every day. At this rate, according to his averages, at the end of the month, allowing for twenty-two working days, he should experience a gain in income of $1,000 as a result of the extra sales his activity would yield.

If you're a salesperson, is your phone call worth $30? Is it worth $100? Or $150? Is seeing a prospect or seeing a client worth $150? Or is it worth $1,000? Sometimes when we know exactly how much value there is in a given activity, we find much greater motivation to carry it out.

A couple of years ago, I worked as a consultant for a Fortune 500 computer company. We worked with the salespeople and sales managers. In our research, we determined that the salespeople were being financially rewarded for making sales, but not for all the activity leading up to the sales. The company agreed to an experiment, which I directed. We slightly decreased sales commissions and instead gave the salespeople $50 for every person they spoke to prospecting for new business. As expected, phone calls increased dramatically, which also increased appointments, which in turn led to increased sales and commissions.

## The Four-Point Index to Averages

Take a sheet of paper and figure out your averages. Use figure 11.1 as a guideline. Start with the initial activity, whether it is making a phone call, jogging, or diet control. If you are a salesperson making a sale, how many appointments does it take before you make a sale? Please write that down.

How many appointments do you book before you actually hold one? When you book an appointment, sometimes you have fall-out—people who call you up and say they can't make it. On the average, how many appointments do you need to book to actually go on a face-to-face interview or physical appointment? How many telephone calls do you make before getting a booked appointment? These telephone calls can be referrals or cold calls. How many of these phone calls do you make to get one booked appointment? Or perhaps, how many doors do you need to knock on before you talk to someone?

Please record these numbers. By doing so, you should have a good idea of exactly how much activity is needed to get one sale. When you see how much activity you must invest to make one sale—how many appointments you need to go on, how many phone calls you need to make—or, in weight loss, how many sodas *not* to indulge in, you will probably be very surprised.

I would like you to calculate the amount of money you could make for each telephone call you complete before making a sale. I'd also like you to calculate the amount of money you make on each appointment you complete before making a sale. Many times this simple exercise—calculating the amount of money we can make at each step of the process, rather than calculating only the amount of money per sale—serves as a very nice motivational lift to help you feel better about the work you are doing right now.

Keep the four-point index to averages handy, perhaps on an index card in your purse or wallet, inside your office drawer, or posted near the phone, so that each time you begin to experience a drop in motivation, you can remind yourself that each call has a dollar value, and some simple multiplication can easily motivate you to get going. If you don't know for sure what your averages are, record your daily activities over a typical week. Remember to keep track of the following:

- How many appointments you hold before making a sale
- How many appointments you book before holding one

- How many telephone calls you need to make to get a sale
- How much money you make per phone call or appointment completed before making a sale

If you are applying this to nonsales goals, record other activities you are doing right that will help you achieve your objective.

I recently worked with an insurance agent who worked for a major firm. His name is Craig. Craig wanted a 650i BMW. Craig's average commission on a sale was approximately $500. He knew that to lease this BMW would cost around $450 a month. Craig also knew that one sale equaled two closing interviews, which equaled about five opening interviews or face-to-face appointments, which in turn equaled five booked appointments (since he had no fallout), which equaled approximately twenty referral calls. Craig realized he needed to increase his activity by $450 every month to pay for this new BMW. This translated into making four extra phone calls, one extra booked appointment, and one face-to-face opening appointment per week, which in turn translated to one closing interview every two weeks and approximately one sale every month, which equaled about $500. Craig was easily able to find out exactly how much effort and work he needed to do to acquire that BMW exactly when he wanted it.

## Less Tangible Goals

Whenever the effort expended is laid out in this manner, with a definite work plan, goals not only seem within reach, but they also seem almost easy to reach. But perhaps your goal is not a physical object, like a BMW. Maybe your goal is something less tangible, like gaining more knowledge about your business. Obviously gaining more knowledge in itself is not a goal. Specifying precisely what you want to know is a goal. Maybe you want more product knowledge. But you must be even more specific, such as deciding you want to learn about new taxation policies. Be even more specific: decide to learn exactly which taxation benefits help your business most in selling your product.

You probably have a good idea how many hours of extra reading you need to do weekly or daily to achieve a given level of competency or knowledgeability about your business. You'll need to specify how many seminars or conferences you plan to attend and by when you want to achieve your goal of becoming more knowledgeable. Decide how much effort you must and will put in over and above your present levels to achieve the goal you want when you want it.

## Where Is Your Effort Going? The 80/20 Rule

If you are a manager or a salesperson who would like to become more productive without using averages, you need to determine where your effort is going.

The 80/20 rule says that, in most cases, 80 percent of our effort results in 20 percent of our productivity. Is this true with you? Is 20 percent of your business growth taking 80 percent of your time?

The 80/20 rule is a very old-line management concept, which leads many industrial psychologists to believe that most people in business are not spending their time and effort effectively; they are not as efficient as they could be in doing the things that make them the most money. If you're a manager, think about the activity or program that yields you the highest business return on investment. Also think about what you have to do to increase your income.

If you're a manager with a set salary and no extra income sources, such as a commission, what do you have to do to increase your income by bonuses, by overrides, or even by promotions?

- Do you need to hire one salesperson a month?
- Do you need to terminate other salespeople?
- Do you need to hold more meetings?
- Do you need more training and development sessions?
- Do you simply need to use better time management techniques?
- Exactly what do you need to do to make yourself more efficient in your business?

I have worked with a number of managers. I recall one in particular, who was hard-working and had a tremendous talent for his type of management of salespeople. But he complained about not having enough time to do the things he needed to do. This is a very typical management complaint. This manager knew he needed to develop new marketing plans but found he spent more than six hours a day solving his salespeople's problems and doing paperwork. He felt guilty and upset that he couldn't accomplish things he knew he had to accomplish, and he also found he had to work more than twelve hours a day to try to make up for the time he spent solving problems.

## What's Your Activity Level?

The overall message here is to get you to determine what you are trying to accomplish in your business. What steps do you need to take to get where you want to be? Besides knowing what your averages are, besides knowing how much you have to work to achieve a sale or another objective, you also need to know some other extremely important information:

- What is your activity level right now?
- What are you spending your time doing?
- Do you know how you are spending your day?

## Keeping a Diary and Journal

A very good way to find out how you're spending your day is to use a diary. In it, you should write down every project you do. You should also write down the number of minutes or hours you spend on it. You want to record how much effort you currently expend on each project. This exercise may prove very embarrassing, since most of us spend too much time doing nonproductive things like chatting with office partners or talking on the phone about personal concerns without realizing that it's taking a big chunk out of our productive day. By keeping this diary you can learn:

- On the average day, how many calls you make
- How many people you see or interview
- How many sales you make during the average week

In addition to the diary, keeping a day-to-day journal is another very important facet of increasing your productivity level. Unlike your diary, in which you list specific activities you've done during the day, your journal is the place for you to write at least one to two paragraphs about your day. This way you can clearly think through the problems you may encounter as you struggle to change your behavior and achieve more productivity.

Writing about your day in the journal helps you think out on paper the reasons you want to change, along with the good things that happen to you during the day. It gives you a daily outlet for your responses to the rewards and punishments you give yourself, and it also gives you a chance to look back on previous days and recall how you felt. You can compare your days and see how much you're changing—and how much better you feel about the behaviors you're trying to change.

Journal writing is something psychologists frequently use in therapy. They usually feel that if a client writes down his or her thoughts and feelings, the client will become more introspective and think more about his or her emotions. If you've ever done any letter writing, even though you don't like to do it, you often find it's kind of fun, because you're able to concentrate deeply on your own emotional aspects of the things you are writing about. More importantly, it brings back a lot of memories, and gives you a chance to think about feelings you usually don't have the time to concentrate on.

Please keep up a daily journal. Try to write at least one paragraph every day you are on this program.

With the diary—in which you record specific activities—you should try to calculate how much activity you're spending on making calls, seeing or interviewing people, and making sales during the day and the week. Use the diary to mark down the number of hours you are doing something or to indicate when you start and finish an activity. Above all else, be as honest as possible. Don't try to inflate your activity levels. If you do, you could become frustrated and discouraged.

## Using the Diary to Know How Hard You Are Working

What you are trying to find out here, basically, is how hard are you currently working? What are you spending your time doing? What results are you getting from all your hard work?

From research over the past five to ten years, we've found that goals are great, but if you don't know how hard you'll have to work for them, they're meaningless. People who write down a goal expect to achieve it. But when it comes time to actually work for that goal, all of the joy is taken out of it. All the great hopes and ambitions dissipate when people finally realize that having a goal means nothing more than just having a direction on which to focus your effort.

## The Secret Is Work

Recently I was in the offices of the Equitable Life Insurance Company of Iowa. While a manager and I were in his office discussing a project, he took out a varnished block of wood with hinges. On top it said, "The Secret to Success." I opened it to find this secret spelled out: "WORK."

Work! Many people, when they find out they have to work hard to achieve their goals, decide that having objectives isn't really that wonderful at all. There's no mystery. There's no secret formula to being successful and getting the things you want. Success comes to those who are willing to work for it. And, perhaps even more importantly, you need to know how hard you'll have to work to achieve the goal.

## Knowledge + Plan = Results

The next step is to lay a plan for achieving your goal based on your own present work habits, and calculate what extra work you need to do to accomplish what you want. Let me give you an example of how this works.

In the late 1970s, the top-ranked male tennis player in the world was Guillermo Vilas. At that time, Vilas had won approximately forty-eight consecutive tennis matches. He was really a killer on the court. He would put away practically every shot, never letting his opponent get more than just a couple of points per game. A real pro, he always went for the jugular every chance he could.

As we were leaving the tennis stadium, we happened upon a little sidewalk café, where I spotted Vilas sitting with his coach, Jan Tiriac. Tiriac was Vilas' motivational dynamo. A Romanian with a Fu Manchu moustache, he was a real driver, a hard-hitter. In fact, during the match, every time Vilas hit a shot out or had trouble handling a serve or a return, he would always look up at Tiriac, and Tiriac, with that big frown of his, kept hitting the chair in front of him, as if Vilas knew exactly what Tiriac meant.

I spotted Vilas having some cappuccino in that sidewalk cafe. I smiled at him and waved. He called us over to share some coffee. After a few minutes of talking about the match, I asked Vilas something I had wondered for years: "Guillermo, how is it that you're such a strong player? How do you win so often and consistently play such great tennis? What gives you that 'killer instinct' to put the ball away and to play so hard?"

What Vilas said was a total surprise to me and, I think, to the other people at the table. He said that he'd rather sniff daisies and read poetry than play tennis. The only reason he got out there was that he just enjoyed the game and it made some money for him.

I wasn't satisfied with that answer. I asked again, "How do you play so well? How do you consistently win so many matches?"

Vilas became serious then, and finally he said, "Kerry, you know there's really no difference between the way I play and the way a low-ranked pro plays. In fact, on any given day, any other pro could probably beat me. But," he continued, "the reason I'm better than some of the other top players on the circuit, the reason I win so much, is that in 1975, I decided my goal was to win the French Open three years later, in 1978. It was a time when my tennis career was really blossoming, yet I wasn't winning any of the great tournaments."

He went on, "Kerry, it's not enough just to decide you want to win a match such as the French Open. I wanted to ensure that I really would win that tournament, so I began planning. In 1977, my goal was to win the Italian Open. In 1976, my goal was to play on the Grand Prix and win tournaments in Munich and also in Rome."

Vilas said he wanted to know positively that he would win all those tournaments. He calculated every month exactly what tournaments he had to win on a world-class circuit. Every week he knew how long he had to practice to win those satellite tournaments in order to ultimately be able to win the world-class tournaments. He set a game plan for himself. He would have practice sessions from 8 in the morning until 12 noon. Then he'd resume from 1 until 5 every day that he didn't have a tournament.

Vilas said the secret of laying a plan like this was merely working backwards from the goal to the present. He knew exactly how much effort he had to put in, how much work he would have to do, to win the French Open in 1978. So he worked backwards and laid a plan for himself that couldn't fail, given his talent and given how hard he was prepared to work. Vilas said, "Kerry, most people spend more time planning a vacation than they do their lives. They spend more time deciding what they want to do on a weekend than to what they want to accomplish during any given month or year."

Think of building a house. You envision the house you want. You decide you want a four-bedroom place with a swimming pool, a veranda, and a good view of the mountains or lake nearby. The architect then takes your ideas—your goal—and translates them into a workable plan, which he calls a blueprint. Can you imagine the builder building without a blueprint—without a game plan? Many times builders do not stay on schedule, but they at least know what they have to do next.

## Laying Your Framework

By the time you finish reading this book, you'll know precisely how productive you are. You'll know how many contacts it takes for you to get an appointment, how many appointments fall through, and even how many times you have to see a client to make a sale. You'll be able to apply this to goals and activities like weight loss or child discipline.

Laying a framework or plan for yourself to achieve a goal is a fundamental element of your productivity program, but there are also other important methods for increasing your productivity. One is finding ways to stay on your game plan. This is the only way any of us can ever hope to achieve anything of substance. In business, when you buy a capital asset, you may borrow money. The bank promptly lays a plan in which, hopefully, you can easily pay back the loan you used to buy that asset.

When using a budget, you understand exactly how much money you need to make per month and per year to survive. You have a good idea of accounts receivables and payables. You know what the break-even points are, as well as the profitability of each sale.

You probably already go into a lot of detail when planning out business goals. Why not use the same approach in your personal life? I recently spoke to a realtor who took part in one of my Peak Performance seminars. He had decided to double his activity, and thereby double the number of sales that he was making.

## The Law of Forced Efficiency

When you work eight hours a day, double your activity, and then double your sales, you will push yourself pretty hard. I met with a realtor after only two weeks on his productivity program. He told me he had become more efficient in listening to his prospects. He tried to make better use of his time, and he was making more referral contacts instead of cold calls. He also said he was attending more seminars on property financing and on marketing development.

In short, he was pushing himself, but at the same time, he found easier ways to achieve the end result of doubling his sales. He used less activity to increase his productivity. He was becoming more efficient and effective at what he was doing.

The law of forced efficiency says the more you force yourself to increase your activity, the more efficient you will become and the more easily money will come to you. Ask yourself these questions:

- What will you do differently to reach your goal?
- What do you need to do to achieve that goal when you want it?

If you're a manager, specify the goal you want to achieve, and write down the amount of time you'll spend on the duties you'll do on a daily basis to achieve that objective.

I also encourage you to remember the law of imminent survival, which states that you'll burn yourself out if you work too hard. You'll lose enthusiasm and interest in your job if you work too many hours trying to achieve an objective. I heartily encourage managers around the country to learn how to be efficiently productive enough to work eight-hour days. There is no glory in working ten to twelve hours a day. It only suggests you aren't sharp enough to delegate and manage the right way.

Try to learn how to leave your work at the office and be effective enough to work a normal day. Just knowing averages and your activity levels is not enough. Knowing how much effort you need to expend to increase your activity and achieve the goal when you want it is only one part. You must also learn ways of maintaining that activity to keep your productivity level high, instead of raising your activity for one or two days and dropping back down to what you had been comfortable with. Keeping that activity high can be accomplished through something called *habit-pattern conditioning*.

Chapter 13—on habits and habit patterns—will give you information, not only about how to condition yourself, but also about how to determine what your habit patterns are, how you can eliminate them, and how you can change virtually anything in your basic work-style to suit the way you would like to perform. You will learn ways not only of conditioning yourself, but also of understanding basic human behavior and why people do what they do.

# Thirteen

# What Stimulates You?

## Habits and Habit Patterns: Your Immediate and Deferred Reward System

Everything we think, do, or say is learned. We learned how to behave by receiving meaningful rewards for exhibiting particular behaviors. To make the changes we want in our behavior so we can achieve greater productivity, it is important to understand the structure of habits and how they can be formed and modified.

### Rewards and Punishments

We work for rewards such as money, recognition, or status. We jog because it feels good or because it gives us firmer bodies and more endurance. We are polite to people because we want them to be polite to us or to like us.

Everything we do results from striving to receive some sort of reward. We try to avoid punishments. Whether it's speeding or parking tickets, we try to avoid any kind of fine associated with vehicular violations, so we abide by traffic codes. We make right turns only when we're supposed to; we park only in designated parking areas; or we drive carefully and obey state laws and rules of the road because we don't want to be fined if a policeman happens to catch us.

A traffic fine is a form of punishment. Our tendency to avoid punishment and seek rewards is the prime psychological motivation for everything we do. Every habit we have was formed by being rewarded for an action or a behavior. Punishment, on the other hand, is the most prevalent technique people use on others to change their habits. But punishment causes resentment and ill feelings. The habit or behavior may change, but only because the person wants to avoid punishment, not because the person really wants to change.

We can try to eliminate habits or behaviors with punishment, but this usually causes resentment, distrust, and anxiety in the person being punished. This is one reason why harsh, disciplinarian, punishment-oriented parents often rear misfits and social dropouts. Their children often avoid the parents. They end up resenting and distrusting not only their authority, but that of other authority figures. If you balance discipline with kindness and warmth, however, they'll probably see other authority figures in society as benign.

## Behavior Shaping

Your parents gave rewards you when you made your bed in the morning by saying, "Thank you," or, when you did your homework, by giving you permission to hang with your friends.

Your parents produced the habit in you of making your bed or doing your homework by giving you praise or by letting you go out and play baseball after you had accomplished the task.

These examples involve behavior shaping. Since adults are really just grown children, the same mechanisms that were used to shape our behaviors as children can be and are used to shape our behaviors as adults. We can also use behavior shaping to get others to act the way we want.

After I give a seminar presentation, the attendees might line up to buy books. This response serves to reward and reinforce whatever I've said during that program. If I told a story during my presentation that they especially liked, and they complimented me on it, the chances of my telling that story again are very high. My attendees are shaping the way I give presentations, or shaping my speaking behavior, by complimenting me and thus rewarding me with praise for the things they like. They might also punish me by telling me they don't like my presentation. Their punishment serves to make me analyze my program and make changes, or perhaps decide not to tell a particular story.

## Environmental Conditioning

Even if we think we are totally self-controlled, we really are slowly being conditioned and manipulated by our environment. Wouldn't it be nice to be able to control yourself the same way your environment is controlling you every day?

Let me give you an example of this. Please complete the following sentences: "Try it, you'll . . ."

If you said, "Like it," you've been conditioned to respond in a predictable way.

Here's another one: "Ask and you shall . . ."

If you thought, "Receive," you've been conditioned to respond with the rest of a particular phrase after you hear a few words.

"Two and two equals . . ."

Your response to this simple equation should be on the tip of your tongue; you've been conditioned to have an immediate response of "four."

Here's another one: "Seven-Up is the un . . ."

Some of this is generational, but if you said "Cola," you've been conditioned by television and other factors in the outside environment.

The responses you gave to the prompts you are examples of habit patterns. In most cases, these patterns, in most cases have been subliminally, or without your conscious knowledge, conditioned in you as an instant reflex.

At this point you're probably feeling that you're being controlled by your environment, by ads, by your friends, by all the things around you—and you're right. Yet without habit patterns, life itself would be virtually impossible.

## The Importance of Habit Patterns

Habit patterns help you make routine decisions. When you get home after a hard day's work, you don't stand in your doorway trying to decide what you should do first. Your habits work to help you walk in, take your jacket off, sit down, and read the newspaper without having to think about it.

Habit patterns are important because they help to keep us productive. Without them, we would be confused much of the time. Just consider the amount of time we would lose if we had to stop and decide what to do first, second, and so on in the morning routine—whether to go to the bathroom first or put on our slippers. Think about your own morning habits. Consider how awkward and confusing it would be to do them out of the sequence you have established over the years.

Habits increase our productivity when we are communicating or interacting with someone. When someone talks to you, you listen. When they're done, you say, "I understand," or "I have a question." You respond, thereby rewarding them by confirming that you were listening. You both don't talk at the same time. You have been conditioned to either listen or speak.

You've also been conditioned by the outside environment to smile when you first meet someone. Another familiar example of a conditioned habit is to respond with "Fine, thank you," when someone asks, "How are you?" These habits actually aid us and increase our productivity by keeping communication channels open and enabling us to have good social skills.

If we didn't have habits, life itself would be extremely dangerous. If we didn't have a conditioned habit pattern when driving a car on a freeway, for example, we might change lanes at the drop of a hat, or turn off the freeway from the left lane when the turnoff is on the right side of the road.

Habit patterns also give our lives social order. We have a good idea of how other people are going to react in situations. In most cases, if we're nice to people, they in turn are nice back. In most cases, we can predict with a fair amount of accuracy that people won't fly off the handle at the drop of a hat and throw things or shoot people. Although there is some evidence that these habit patterns break down with psychotic or schizophrenic individuals, by and large if we smile at somebody, they'll smile back. If we frown at somebody, they'll frown back. Habits help us function smoothly in our lives. They help us lead productive, predictable lives. They prevent confusion.

## The Roots of Habit Patterns

Habits are extremely tough to break, mainly because they're tough to form. The whole process of change or modifying habits is one of the most difficult things we can ever do. The change causes stress and thereby discomfort.

Most of us fail to stick to our New Year's resolutions largely because of the anxiety brought about by change when we start to modify our habits. When I played professional tennis, for example, I had a very smooth, very accurate backhand, but it wasn't always that way. When I was learning how to play tennis at the age of five, I had an enormous problem learning both the forehand and backhand, and at the ages of eight and nine, I remember hitting with my backhand sometimes as much as two to three hours a day. At a young age, that's a very high amount of activity.

But after about two to three months of practicing hard at hitting my backhand, muscle memory came into play. I didn't have to concentrate on getting my racket low, leading with my shoulder, moving into the ball. All those things came very naturally without my having to even think about them.

In time, just like muscle memory, habits tend to become entrenched. Of course our entrenched habit patterns can sabotage our efforts in working toward an objective. How are habit patterns formed? To answer this, you'll need to know a little about human behavior.

## Human Behavior Results from Rewards and Punishments

As we saw earlier, human behavior results from rewards and punishments. We all tend to seek rewards for activities we do, and we all tend to flee from punishment. If you had a girlfriend or boyfriend who was appreciative, complimentary, and affectionate, you would want to be around them often. You may buy things to indicate you like them. You may be as nice as you can be to that special person.

If this person told you that you were a jerk whenever you made a mistake, or was constantly deprecating you, you would probably try to replace the person within a very short time. When the person was complimentary, or rewarded you, they caused you to feel more accepted and closer in the relationship, because you seek rewards just as you seek to avoid punishment or people who are inflicting it.

Rewards and punishments affect almost every aspect of our lives. If we go to a grocery store, and it is constantly crowded, we'll probably go to another. We find the crowds of the grocery store aversive or punishing. We tend to avoid such situations.

Every habit we currently have was formed by being rewarded for an action. If you brought doughnuts to your secretary one morning, and she not only told you how much she liked you bringing them but also worked harder and more efficiently, you would probably bring donuts every morning from then on. You would create a habit in yourself of bringing those donuts to work. In time, you would instill new work habits in your secretary by rewarding her.

## Parental Rewards and Peer Reinforcement

When you were a child, your habits were established by your parents with rewards and by your peers with peer reinforcement. Think back for a moment. If your peer group used words like "cool," didn't you also use these words because you wanted to be accepted by your group? They in turn would reward you by letting you be a part of their group.

As children, our habits were constantly established or changed by peer reinforcement. We all wore the same type of T-shirts. All of our friends wore Levis, so we wore Levis too. Or we wore the same brand of tennis shoes.

The reward, or reinforcement, was acceptance from our peer group. We wanted them to like us. They showed they did like us as a reward for dressing, acting, or speaking like a part of the group.

Parents also reinforced our behaviors or rewarded habits when we were very young by giving us an allowance or a reward for mowing the lawn or cleaning our room. Receiving fifty cents for mowing the lawn once a week made it more likely that you would also mow the lawn the next week and the week after that, or do the dishes one night, or rake the leaves. Soon a habit pattern would be established. Even if you didn't receive the allowance as often, you would still mow the lawn or rake the leaves in anticipation of the reward.

Many parents use rewards with their children very appropriately. One parent I know occasionally buys her son a favorite toy just because he sweeps the driveway daily. This random reward works well because the mother tells the child why he is getting the toy. Since he never knows when to expect it, he tends to sweep the driveway daily, anticipating he might be rewarded with a toy.

## Intermittent, Immediate, and Deferred Rewards

In real life, intermittent rewards are prevalent in places like casinos. Slot machines are one of the most addictive vices around. One reason for this is that when we use a slot machine, we're rewarded when three oranges or three lemons come up on the window. The machine gives us ten times the amount of money we put in. It does not reward us every time we put another quarter in, but perhaps every tenth, twentieth, or even one hundredth time. This intermittent reward is enough to keep us playing that machine. You always feel that the next time will be your big win.

Receiving an intermittent reward keeps us gambling. In many cases it establishes a habit. If you see a slot machine and think you will try it "just once," chances are you will keep feeding coins in the slot. We do things to get immediate rewards, like getting a point every time we win in a tennis game. We also work for deferred rewards, such as the revenue yielded by a long-term investment after a year or two. Both types of rewards can be used to establish, modify, or break habits. The more immediately we receive a reward us for an activity, the greater the chance the activity will become a habit. That's because we basically tend to do activities that give us the most immediate rewards.

For example, if you bought your spouse roses and as soon as you presented them you received a kiss, you would probably do it again. But if you presented the roses and it took a week or two before you were told how nice they were, you probably wouldn't buy roses anymore, or at least not very frequently.

Many of us avoid doing things that give us deferred rewards, like starting a new business. Businesses usually have an initial start-up period of about two years. Most individuals don't make it in business partly because they don't have the patience to wait for rewards such as high income, freedom, and less work: it takes so long to get these things. They have made the mistake of only setting the goal—establishing a business—without planning the steps to get there, the work they must do to get the goal, and the rewards they might receive along the way.

Salespeople usually dislike prospecting or digging up new business on the telephone. If the salesperson can receive an immediate reward, however, such as eating a piece of a favorite candy or fruit or some other treat after each phone call is made, those calls become less disliked and more enjoyable. They also become much closer to a habit, because making the phone call is rewarded by receiving a piece of candy or fruit.

A short time ago, I worked with a salesperson at a major stock brokerage company who intensely disliked prospecting. He disliked it to the point that, even though his business was sinking so badly that he probably wasn't going to survive in the investment industry, he still wouldn't make referral calls or cold calls.

I asked him what he liked to eat. He told me he enjoyed bananas. So I got the idea of linking the reward of one small piece of banana to every phone call made. He told me that about a month later, after using the banana as a reward, his cold calls and referral calls increased 150 percent. Every time he made a phone call, he'd give himself a small piece of banana, so he was really working for the bite of fruit. Nonetheless, he still was able to associate a pleasurable experience, such as eating the fruit, with a nonpleasurable experience like the phone call. Making the phone calls began to be much more enjoyable.

Most of us don't enjoy directly prospecting or making phone calls because the people we call often aren't nice or very polite to us.

But if we give ourselves a reward for doing this undesirable activity, we can usually increase the amount of phone calls we make.

Rewards can be applied in virtually any situation where we want to change habits or modify behavior. My son has a problem picking up his toys. He leaves toys in the living room and scattered about his bedroom. Since asking him to pick up his toys doesn't work, and yelling at him has an equally useless effect, we started him on a program in which he receives 25 cents as a reward every day that he picks up all his toys without being asked. This reward of 25 cents is a tremendously effective technique. It establishes and solidifies his habit of picking up his toys. This only works, however, because he places money at a very high value he can buy what he wants with the money and not have to ask us for toys. He has the freedom to purchase what he wants. If you want to cause a behavior to become a habit, reward yourself for the behavior after you do it.

## Promoting Behaviors into Habits

If we can engage in an activity, such as making prospecting calls consistently for three to four weeks—twenty-one to twenty-eight days—it will become a habit. But new behaviors must be done on a regular basis.

Habits work against us too. Most of us don't realize that if we go to work late—perhaps five or ten minutes every day for one month straight—a habit will form. It will set in much as molding putty sets and dries. It's very difficult to change the shape of the putty once it dries, just as it's difficult to change a habit once it's established. Bad habits are much easier to start or initiate than they are to break.

Some psychological researchers say that habits are never really broken; we just put new habits in their place. Doing anything repeatedly for twenty-one to twenty-eight days is really all it takes to put a new habit in place. For example, I enjoy reading very much. It's also crucial to my business. But I usually find it very difficult to take the time to read. To encourage this activity, I reward myself, usually in the evening, with small sips of root beer, which I also enjoy very much. This root beer acts as a reinforcer or a reward. I used the reward of getting the sip of root beer for every page turned for approximately twenty-one days. After this period, even though I didn't drink the root beer anymore when I reading, I developed a habit of reading nightly. The habit solidified within that three-week period, and I continued to read almost every night from then on, even without the root beer. If I wasn't able to read, I felt that I had missed something that day, as you would feel if you hadn't brushed your teeth before going to bed at night.

The only way to change or modify our habit patterns is to use a reward-based conditioning technique like the one I've been describing.

## Eliminating Habits with Punishment

A habit is eliminated if you receive punishment for it. If you received an electric shock when you put your key in the front door of your home, it wouldn't be long before you'd use the back door. Or if the roses you brought home to your spouse went unacknowledged or were ill-received, it wouldn't be long before you stopped bringing roses, and probably stopped bringing presents in general.

It's very difficult for a behavior to become a habit or stay a habit if you receive no enjoyment when you do it. At the same time, if you are laughed at, embarrassed, or reprimanded when you take part in it, the habit won't last long. Punishment does not help form habits, but it helps break them.

Think of speeding down the highway in your car. This is extremely dangerous as well as not very fuel-efficient. In time, speeding becomes a habit. Soon you would probably feel that driving slowly was boring. Fortunately, the habit of speeding is dealt with very effectively by highway-patrol officers. They punish you by giving traffic tickets. Eventually a traffic-court judge will punish you with a fine. If you find it fun to speed again, you are called a repeat offender (this really means that you are not responding well to punishment), who is dealt with by imposing stricter and higher fines, perhaps even jail. The authorities give you tougher and tougher punishments, hoping that they will eliminate your habit of speeding.

Punishment, or not getting a reward for a habit, is very useful in eliminating habits or behavior patterns, but not at all useful in forming habits. For example, if your spouse has a habit of leaving the car lights on when returning home, complaining will probably stop him or her from the habit of leaving the lights on. But he or she will also probably intensely resent your chiding; it'll cause marital strife; and your spouse may even think of ways to get back at you for your scolding or condescending behavior.

If, on the other hand, you give your spouse a reward for remembering to turn the lights off—perhaps a hug or kiss or doing some extra household chores—not only would you shape a habit of turning the lights off, but your spouse would also probably enjoy being with you much more and would show it through happiness or gratitude.

Although punishment does work to eliminate certain behaviors and habits, rewards usually work twice as fast in forming new ones. As noted earlier, habits are not really eliminated, but rather replaced. The same thing is true with children. If your child runs outside without putting on a jacket on a cold day, screaming at the child will probably work: it will probably keep the child from going out without a jacket. But you'll probably have to scream each time. By giving your child a reward, such as praise, affection, or candy, for putting on a jacket, the child will grow up to be much happier, better-adjusted, and more confident, and will possess higher self-esteem. The child will also be much more loving, affectionate, and admiring of you as the parent.

Punishment may have its place, but it's used much too often to eliminate habits or change behaviors. Rewards work much more effectively, if only because the basic end of punishment is really to enable the punisher to vent his or her anger or frustration.

Punishment never has formed and never will form a habit pattern. A husband might say to his wife, "Why don't you have dinner on the table when I come home? I don't know why I ever married you." He should know that criticism only causes distress, anger, and rejection in his wife, but does not serve to change her behavior.

Parents often tend to make the great mistake of using punishment to try to reinforce and establish behaviors: "Tommy, why can't you ever learn to tie your own shoes?" You can probably sense why anxiety, rejection, and discouragement set in, making it likely that Tommy will avoid tying his shoes appropriately, as well as feeling dislike and anxiety toward his parents.

Consider two things:

1. Are you spending too much time punishing others—your family and friends—for inappropriate behavior instead of rewarding them for appropriate behavior?

2. Are you punishing or rewarding yourself?

Punishing yourself can be even more devastating than having someone else do it to you. In 1978, when I was on the Grand Prix Tennis Tour, frequently, in the middle of a tennis match, I would berate myself. I couldn't deal with my own bad shots. But when I was in Monte Carlo in Europe, I was able to play the number 3 rated tennis player from Argentina. We were playing on a clay-court surface, which I wasn't used to. Being from California, I was used to a fast serve and a volley game on a hard-court surface. Every time I missed a ball, I'd say to myself, "You idiot! Can't you do anything right?" Every time I'd miss, I'd get angrier and more upset. But as you might have guessed, the more agitated I became, the worse I played. There tends to be a snowball effect, until you finally do exactly as you predicted you would—poorly. It becomes a self-fulfilling prophecy: "Kerry! I knew you couldn't hit that ball."

I was losing. But then I decided to change tactics. In the middle of the second set of a three-set match, I stopped punishing myself for my bad shots. I began by giving myself a sip of water every time I hit a winner. I'd go to the sidelines very briefly and take a sip of water, and then go right back onto the court.

While this was a bit irregular, because it slowed down the tennis match, I found that by giving myself rewards or reinforcements, my confidence was built up. I also played better. I started congratulating myself. I started giving myself encouragement for the good shots that I made while ignoring the bad ones.

## Increasing Performance with Rewards

You can increase your performance if you reward rather than punish yourself. This will build self-confidence instead establishing how bad or worthless you are. The foundation of your whole sales and business performance really rests on building self-esteem and self-confidence. It's important to understand basic human behavior, habits, and habit patterns before you can ever attempt to make any changes in yourself. By understanding how you influence and control others with rewards and punishments and how they control you, the next chapters—on discriminative stimuli, the psychology of change, and how you can modify your own behavior to increase your performance—will be much more meaningful. You'll have clearer insight into potential sales performance barriers and know how you can remove them.

By the time you finish reading this book, you'll have enough information to create a reward-based conditioning technique that can help you vastly increase the amount of money you are now making. You can even apply these concepts to losing weight or becoming a better parent. You'll virtually be able to condition a change in any habit or behavior you choose. Most important, if you follow your tailor-made performance program, your business will increase dramatically within eight weeks.

# Fourteen
# How Good Are You?

## Analyzing and Comparing Current Production to Future Needs

Are there times when you feel depressed for no apparent reason? Or do you feel anxious or nervous in certain situations, like speaking in front of groups, but feel fine meeting one-on-one? Do you feel strange , upset, or anxious when walking into your office or sitting at your desk after a long vacation?

On the other hand, do you get a comfortable, warm feeling as soon as you get home after a long day? Does your mood change as soon as you step into the doorway of your house? Does your spouse greet you with a smile and a kiss? Or do your kids immediately give you a hug and tell you how much they love you?

Why do our emotions change drastically just because we're in a different environment? Even without verbal interaction, why do we feel good or even suspicious there?

### Discriminative Stimulus

In my work, I've heard businesspeople say, "I felt uncomfortable as soon as I walked into his office. I don't know what it was, but I felt very ill at ease," or "It was one of the warmest places I've ever been. I couldn't spot anything different about his office than anybody else's, but it was just a place I wanted to get back to."

The difference lies in the psychological explanation called a *discriminative stimulus*, or environmental conditioning, which we discussed briefly in chapter 13. The underlying idea of discriminative stimuli is that our feelings of comfort or discomfort with people like lawyers, or in places like highways or offices, depend on our previous experience.

If we have worked only with lawyers who have been demeaning or condescending or have made us feel subhuman, we will become conditioned to feel uncomfortable as soon as we step into a lawyer's office. If we have had a difficult problem at one time with a particular lawyer—perhaps he or she made us feel stupid—we probably came away from that meeting feeling that we didn't want to see this lawyer—or any lawyer—again. If we go into another lawyer's office the following week, our feelings of discomfort will probably still be there. Our feelings will start to become generalized. We will start to feel uncomfortable in any lawyer's office. Even though another lawyer has said nothing more than "Hello, how are you?" our last experience will easily arouse our suspicion and apprehension.

The opposite may be true of our homes. If we feel sudden joy or comfort as soon as we walk into our house, it's probably because our spouses makes us feel wonderful, like a special person, even though they may not even be around when we open the door. We still remember the good feelings of being in the house, which is a strong contrast to the anxiety we experience from a hard day at work.

If our spouse doesn't give us joy, and we still feel good being home, our reaction is a little bit more complex. Home is probably just the lesser of two evils—the greater evil being the daily rigor of work. Even though home may not an especially nice place to be, we still feel better there than we do taking the knocks at the office all day long.

## Overcoming Irrational Fears

Understanding how discriminative stimuli and environmental conditioning work can give us insight into why we often feel distressed or anxious about making calls or going to somebody's office. We can begin to understand that we really are just conditioned to feel distressed by our experience.

Simple stress management techniques can help you cope with stress and anxiety and get rid of your irrational fears, which may have resulted from environmental conditioning.

Let's say, for example, that yesterday, Monday, you made ten phone calls, but with each one you experienced severe rejection. Today is Tuesday, and if you still can't get up enough enthusiasm or motivation to make more phone calls, you have probably been environmentally conditioned by Monday's rejection to anticipate feeling rejected whenever you're around the phone, maybe even whenever you approach your desk.

A good solution in this case might be, after making a phone call to a prospect, immediately calling your spouse or a good friend as a reward. If this produces comfort, it will help decrease anxiety. It will also drive down your chances of feeling rejected. If meeting in a lawyer's or an accountant's office makes you anxious, doing something as simple as getting a milkshake on your way home or stopping off at a friend's office could help relieve the stress or anxiety.

We all feel distress in certain locations or around things that remind us of problems or situations that gave us anxiety. When we experience this distress again, we need to rid ourselves of it so we don't generalize and associate it with similar places or things.

## Using Rewards: De-stressing Techniques

Knowing about environmental conditioning can help you overcome the fears and anxieties you may be experiencing in your business.

I worked with one salesperson who experienced call reluctance even when calling existing customers. (See chapter 9 for more on overcoming call reluctance.) He had become environmentally conditioned by past bad experiences of picking up the telephone. He even felt anxious and distressed just looking at the phone. But by giving himself rewards for making calls, as well as calling friends or acquaintances in between calls, he was able to dissipate his fear and increase his phone activity. He was basically preventing anxiety. He now makes ten referral calls a day. He is even qualifying properly. That instrument of terror, the telephone—the tool that had given him such anxiety in the past—is now something he can cope with.

He de-stressed himself by talking to a friend in between prospect calls. Sometimes he would just chat with an office mate. By doing this he was able to dispel his fear of the telephone and call reluctance.

I worked on an interesting case with a husband who was having great difficulty developing any enthusiasm being around his wife. The individual, a manager in a very prestigious firm, had been married for two or three years. Every time he went home, he felt like going to sleep. He felt little ambition or motivation to do anything with his wife or even to talk to her. This had not always been the case. In fact, he confided to me that during the first year of marriage, all he wanted to do was talk about what had happened during the day. They both spent every evening talking about plans or concerns they had for the future.

The husband told me that after this first year, he and his wife had had a series of terrible confrontations in which she had screamed and thrown things at him. He had reacted similarly to her. After about six months, the marital conflicts died out, but he was left with a feeling of lethargy whenever he was around her. He had been conditioned by their frequent arguments and fights to avoid his wife. When he was around her, he would be quiet. He avoided going out of his way to engage her for fear that the arguments would once again erupt.

Even though he said he wanted to pay more attention to her, and felt much warmer toward her than he had during that six-month conflict period, he still had great difficulty finding any joy in her presence.

This is a classic case of environmental conditioning. For a period of time, the man had received so much punishment and stress from one person that it became difficult for him to engage, even though he felt he wanted to be positive, friendly, even loving toward her.

I once counseled a woman who had difficulty being around tall men with dark hair and dark moustaches. She told me that she had an extremely bad relationship with a man who was tall and had dark hair and a moustache. The relationship had ended when he began physically abusing her. She had been in the hospital for two or three days because of abrasions on her face and bruises and lacerations on her body.

From then on, even in business, she was extremely suspicious of that look, to the point she didn't like to be in the room or an office alone with a man with those characteristics. Her environmental conditioning caused her to generalize her discomfort to a whole group of men.

We are environmentally conditioned in our offices by experiences with the telephone, with clients, and with other professionals, such as lawyers and accountants. At home we are environmentally conditioned by our families.

Often people who are environmentally conditioned will generalize. If we have had a bad experience with the president of a company, other experiences with company presidents will cause avoidance behavior. We all do this type of generalizing. We fear the same experience will materialize again.

We can overcome an environmentally conditioned response by using some simple relaxation or stress-coping techniques, such as rewarding ourselves with reinforcers when we begin to overcome the generalized fears, or by using the progressive-relaxation technique described in chapter 8. Progressive relaxation can help relieve tension caused by anxiety-producing situations.

# Fifteen

# Applying Rewards to the Game Plan

## Changing Target-Production Behavior Patterns

In chapter 13, we talked about how our habits and habit patterns develop from being rewarded for particular behavior patterns. Here you will learn how rewards and reinforcers can be used to help reach target behavior patterns on the road to great performance.

The law of effect holds that we are governed by the consequences of our behavior. We tend to engage in behaviors that yield rewards again and again. If the consequences are unrewarding, we tend to cease from engaging in that behavior.

### Rewards and Reinforcers

Psychologists claim that two types of rewards affect our behavior. Simple rewards are behaviors such as eating, sleeping, and sex. Complex rewards are things like children's toys, praise, attention, compliments, as well as cars and money.

Complex rewards are very powerful, but they may be extremely difficult to recognize, because they vary in effectiveness from person to person. One salesperson may make lots of phone calls because he enjoys phone calls and thinks they are rewarding. Another may make them because he wants to avoid the punishment of his manager threatening termination. It could also be that the salesperson realizes that she'll make a bigger sale—her reward—if she makes those phone calls now.

Some rewards are reinforcing for practically everyone, but the reason some individuals desire a particular reward is sometimes a mystery.

Whether something is a reward or reinforcer depends on a number of things. How important is that reward? How do we feel at the time we receive it? Who is giving the reward? For example, a reward of $50 every time you make a marketing phone call will greatly enhance your chances of making another call. That reward has a high degree of importance and will directly relate to how much you want that money. On the other hand, if you receive a grape or candy bar after every phone call, you will soon become satiated with those rewards. They will become less reinforcing, and it won't be long before you stop making the calls.

The reward obviously needs to be important. It also needs to be frequent. Once you've received a reward for one activity, however, it will directly affect the type of reward you desire for other activities as well. I travel around the country a lot. While I'm away, my wife, Merita, dispensed her own system of rewards and punishments to our children. When Merita asked our daughter Catherine to wash the car, for instance, she would usually give her $10, since that is what she would have paid at the local car wash. For an eleven-year-old, $10 in one hour was more money than most of her friends made in one week. My payment was not as high as wife's. When I asked Catherine to mow the lawn, for example, I would offer $2 or $2.50. She countered, "Why should I mow the lawn for a couple of bucks when I can wait a week and wash Mom's car again?" Often I had to threaten her with punishment to accept the reward.

My youngest daughter, Caroline, didn't like to read and needed to enhance her reading ability. I once offered to reward her with $10 for every book she read. Because Mom's reward payment schedule was higher for jobs Caroline did around the house, an investment of the time to read a book for $10 seemed too much. Because they frequently got money as a reward, the importance of small bills to Catherine and Caroline wasn't that great.

This phenomenon frequently occurs in business. When a salesperson is used to making high commissions but feels stifled in the job, he may have a difficult time moving to a new position. This occurs largely because most sales jobs start out on a base salary or a draw. The salesperson first has to learn the product and market, as well as the potential clients. This is a lot of effort and investment without much reward, and his income may well be lower. Since the frequency at which he received money from his previous job was very high, he does not see the new job as rewarding enough to make the initial sacrifice.

Rewards have an extremely high amount of control over our basic behavior. As I have mentioned, when I speak in front of a group and they all smile or laugh when I use some humor, the chances are increased that I will again use the same joke at a future program. The audience, in essence, has control over what I say to them.

In many cases, an audience can make or break a program. A responsive audience rewards a speaker, helping him or her feel more at ease. A defensive audience produces a poor program by not showing emotion, causing a speaker to feel inhibited or ill at ease and giving a less than excellent presentation. Responsive audiences get a better performance from any speaker.

Similarly, parents often inadvertently reinforce inappropriate behaviors in their children. A small child may be crying in bed. The parents want the child to sleep but pick her up to keep her from crying. The parents have reinforced the child's behavior of crying when she is ill at ease or in bed.

My daughter Stacey manipulated my wife in much the same way. To keep Stacey from crying, Merita would lie down with her until little Stacey fell asleep. Then Mom would walk out of the bedroom and go back to what she had been doing. At three years old, Stacey was fully able to sleep without Mom being with her. Unfortunately, Merita produced a behavior pattern whereby Stacey couldn't fall asleep unless Mom slept with her for at least an hour beforehand.

No wonder salespeople dislike paperwork so much. There are rewards for making sales, but none for filling out the reports needed to keep track of productivity. Recently I consulted with an agency that had problems getting salespeople to send in their reports. My recommendation was to reward the reps for producing reports on time. The company would have a beer party every Friday after work. Only those reps who hit paperwork expectations would be able to attend. Reports were not only turned in on time but were filled out much more efficiently.

One of the most interesting facets of behavioral psychology is the strange phenomenon that when rewards are given infrequently, they can have a more powerful effect on behavior than if they are given out every time the desired behavior occurs. This phenomenon involves a concept called *variable-ratio reinforcement*.

Variable-ratio reinforcement occurs in almost every walk of life. My assistant Marilyn realized that if she did a good job, she would be praised. Unfortunately, I am fairly inconsistent in my praise, but it turned out to the best advantage of the business. When she did a good job and I noticed it, I praised her, which increased the likelihood that she would do a good job on similar projects again. She never knew when she would get praised. She only knew that the praise was random and based on doing a good job.

We talked about two types of rewards in chapter 13: immediate and deferred. With immediate rewards, the more quickly you are given a reward, the greater the chance it has to affect your behavior. For example, if I work for a company and it results in immediate praise within minutes of completing the project, the chances I'll work on a similar project again are very high. If the praise or money for that work takes months or even years to get, I will avoid similar projects in the future.

Most state lottery commissions are very aware of this phenomenon. Decades ago, California had something called the Daily Number. Players had to wait until the evening news to learn if their number had been selected. This is a deferred reward. When sales of lottery tickets sank, the state commission implemented an immediate reward. They began selling scratch-off tickets, whereby players made the purchase, scratched the ticket, and got an immediate reward or (in the case of a wasted expenditure) immediate punishment.

The clerk where any winning ticket was purchased was awarded $5, $10, $25, or even $100 on the spot. The California commission found that sales increased dramatically because of a reward's immediacy.

Deferred rewards can also be very effective, but they must be of very great importance or value to the recipient. When I first started my business, I had to make an enormous number of sales calls. The resulting reward of booking a speech would take days or weeks. I would motivate myself with immediate rewards such as a sip of coffee or grapes or strawberries after every phone call.

I also gave myself a deferred reward to stay on track. If I made enough phone calls during the day, I would reward myself in the evening with a game of tennis, one of my favorite pastimes. While tennis wasn't as valuable as a speaking fee or commission, I would still withhold tennis time unless I earned it. I fully realized that if I didn't make the phone calls, my business would never take off. But I didn't have the discipline to make those calls without a immediate reward mechanism.

Sometimes deferred rewards can be too far removed for the recipient to find them motivating. For example, many companies offer sales-incentive trips in an effort to get people to produce. In January, they may announce an incentive of a free trip to Spain, Hong Kong, or Mexico, to take place the following December, if the salespeople reach a certain production level. Management assumes that the salespeople will produce more during the intervening twelve months because they will want to go on the trip.

Often, however, the salespeople don't even think about the incentive trip until October, when it may be too late to produce enough business to qualify. Rarely will a salesperson produce enough during the months of January to March for a trip that takes place the following December. The reward is deferred too far to have any effect on behavior. Sales-incentive campaigns or contests lasting one to three months are more effective.

Laboratory studies have discovered decreased motivation correlated with deferred rewards. A rat was put into a cage and tested to find out how often it would press a lever to receive a food pellet. If a rat was scheduled to receive a pellet for every nine presses, an interesting thing would happen. It would lackadaisically press the lever four times, but then press it very quickly the last three times. This occurred in almost every case with a predictable reward. It was almost as if the rat could count how many times it would have to push the lever. People behave much the same way. They often procrastinate on a revenue-producing activity until the last minute. Then they work their butts off to meet the quota and get a deferred reward.

## Superstitions

Researchers have also observed that when there was a long delay after the rat pressed the lever before it got its food rewards, or when the reward or reinforcement schedule was complex, the rats would engage in ritualistic behavior patterns; for example, it would do a flip or walk around in a circle. The rat would work this into what is known as a *schedule of reinforcement*.

Our business practices are much the same. We develop ritualistic behaviors or superstitions. We all have seen baseball players approach the batter's box by digging their spikes into the turf in a particular way, then spinning the bat precisely the same number of times before setting for the pitch.

When I was on the professional tennis tour in the late 1970s, I was told that Jimmy Connors would wear socks of a particular color whenever he played John McEnroe. Ivan Lendl would wear only a specific style of shirt when he played Boris Becker. This was based on a prior win against Becker while Lendl was wearing that type of shirt. He associated winning with the shirt and would wear it every time he played Becker in the future. As a popular beer commercial states, "It's not superstition if it works."

When I played tennis on tour, I would tie my shoes a certain way because I had won matches before with that behavior pattern. Forty years ago, when I played in a major tournament in La Jolla, California, I had a major win against a superior player. There was no logical explanation for my 6–3, 6–2 victory other than the opponent just had a bad day. But afterward I evaluated everything I wore, every step I took, and the type of serves I took, trying to pinpoint that exact behavior so I could replicate it in the future. For years after, I made sure that my racket string tension was exactly 58, because that was the tension that helped me defeat that player. This was linked along with bouncing the ball exactly two times before first serve and one time before a second serve.

I still have the ball-bouncing ritual in my tennis behavior. It is extremely difficult to get rid of ritualistic behavior. I recently tried to bounce the ball once for a first serve and was so preoccupied with the discomfort that I ended up double-faulting.

## Relationships

The same law of effect has an impact on relationships. The amount of positive reinforcement or punishment you receive in a relationship to a large extent determines the likelihood of staying together. When the costs of a relationship or marriage outweigh the benefits, there is a greater chance of a breakup.

I recently asked a friend of mine why he broke up with his wife. At first he told me they just didn't get along together, that they both had changed. But in delving deeper, he told me that the reasons for staying together just didn't seem that important. The punishment he experienced far outweighed the rewards and reinforcers in the relationship.

One goal of a relationship is to increase the amount of positive reinforcement we receive from and give to our mate. To outweigh the punishment, or cost, of a relationship, we need to keep increasing the number of rewards or benefits we give to and receive from that relationship.

Sometimes people stay in bad relationships because of good memories. But memories themselves tend to serve as reinforcers. They serve as rewards for staying in the relationship, outweighing some of its bad points. Moreover, people sometimes stay in bad relationships simply because they believe that the cost of breaking up outweigh the negatives of staying in.

Many psychologists believe that we select our friends based on reinforcement. If a friend is complimentary, we feel good. We tend to want to be with them more often. On the other hand, if a friend is not very attentive and rarely compliments, we tend to decrease the amount of time we spend with them. This can extend to your work. If your job as a salesperson or sales manager is rewarding, you tend to stay in it.

Rewards, unfortunately, do change. Financial rewards, while generally good reinforcers, can eventually be taken for granted. As your needs change, so do your financial goals.

Take, for example, an insurance company for which I consulted. The manager of a branch office made about $400,000 a year, but he was extremely dissatisfied. He really wanted to run his own company. The level of emotional punishment he experienced by not running his own business outweighed the reward and reinforcement of a high income. So he left one of the best jobs within the New York Life Insurance Company. His goals had changed. He wanted his own business.

It is very important to evaluate which reinforcers are effective for you. Money is a limited reinforcer. It works for only some people, and only for some of the time.

## Punishment

We stressed earlier that punishment should be avoided when trying to create a behavior. Punishment can weaken a behavior. In other words, if, in the process of making phone calls, you ceased to receive any appointments (rewards), it wouldn't take long before you found making the calls to be a punishing experience. Ultimately, you would stop making those calls.

You can also receive punishment by having normal and natural rewards withheld. For example, a guy I know had a beer in the evening before dinner. He found that not having his beer was a punishing experience.

Punishment works extremely fast; it can also have side effects. Anyone who has been fired from a job or even reprimanded knows that punishment can cause anxiety as well as a long-term decrease in self-esteem and self-confidence. Punishing experiences can reinforce self-sabotaging fears and limit productivity.

Almost every cat lover knows if a cat accidently steps on a hot stove, not only will it never step on another hot stove again, but it won't step on a cold stove either. In many cases, similar avoidance behaviors occur when a salesperson has a bad experience with a prospect. If the experience was punishing enough, there is a strong likelihood that the rep will avoid that kind of prospect in the future.

Punishment can occur both from a negative experience and from not receiving an expected reward. Either can destroy discipline. Motivational speakers may tell you that prospects don't reject you, they reject the product. But this does not make it any easier to accept the rejection (the punishment). Almost all of us every day feel personally rejected when someone says no. One of the best ways to get over the punishment is to minimize the punishment of the rejection and maximize the reward.

One of the biggest problems salespeople have is that many rewards are deferred too long and the rejection is too immediate. I consulted at a real-estate company a few years ago. The manager did what, in my opinion, was a brilliant thing. He realized there was a better than 90 percent chance that his new salespeople would feel so rejected in sales calls that they would soon quit. He wanted to give these salespeople rewards that would far outweigh any punishment they received prospecting for listings. He amortized the average commission over the number of prospective client contacts it took to get a sale. He realized that each prospective client contact the new real-estate agent made was worth approximately $10. So he paid them $10 for every call. As you might have guessed, sales increased by 120 percent. The attrition rate dropped to only about 50 percent. Obviously giving them an immediate reward for a call to a prospective client was much more gratifying than the rejection was punishing.

This book focuses on encouraging you to create rewards that are sufficiently gratifying and fulfilling that they outweigh any punishing situation you can experience in your selling career. You can use these psychological techniques to turn even the worst rejection into beneficial rewards and reinforcers.

## Extinction

A by-product of punishment called *extinction* can actually kill your career. Extinction occurs when we consistently fail to receive an expected reward. Its effect can be more far-reaching than any other form of punishment, because we will often refuse to engage in that behavior ever again.

Above I described lab rats pressing a lever to get food pellets. When a rat is given a food pellet in a fixed-activity format of every three or four presses on the lever, it would keep pressing the lever until it was satiated. But when a food pellet failed to travel down the chute after the usual number of presses, the lack of reward would be punishing to the rat. If, on a fixed-reinforcement schedule of four presses, the rat did not receive a food pellet by the thirteenth press, extinction would occur—it would no longer even try to press the lever.

The same concept holds true in sales. Salespeople often find it difficult to adapt to new products and services. Change is consistent, and even experienced salespeople often meet with resistance from prospects and customers. If punishment occurs often (rejection), behavioral extinction also happens. The salesperson gives up.

Individuals who leave sales often have been punished into extinction. I frequently meet realtors who have gone into other businesses. Recently I met a saleswoman with a major phone provider. I had first met her a year earlier, when she was selling real estate. When I asked her why she quit, she simply said she didn't enjoy the career. She wasn't being reinforced and rewarded in the real-estate business. It had become extinct for her. She'd received so much punishment that she no longer made any connection between trying to sell real estate and the rewards she could have received.

## Increasing Activity

While all of us have set habit patterns, we are also continually establishing or extinguishing new habits. Every day we learn every day how to be successful—or how to fail.

Take the basic idea of rewards and punishments that we've discussed. By giving yourself a reward after a cold call, for example, you decrease your dislike of the telephone and help establish cold calling into a habit. You can take control by using rewards to establish habits to increase your business performance, instead of letting your habits control you.

I consulted with stockbrokers at a New York brokerage company who had great difficulty prospecting for business. One broker in particular was having a hard time calling referred leads. I wanted to find out what his rewards were. He told me that he especially liked hot chocolate. He usually had a cup every evening. Since he enjoyed drinking hot chocolate, we used it as a reinforcer to get him to make his referral phone calls. In fact, his goal was to make approximately ten referral calls each evening, which would usually give him about two booked appointments. His behavior of making referral calls was rewarded with hot chocolate. After every call he made, he would receive a sip of hot chocolate. It was just enough to give him a nice-tasting reward, and he also felt very good about the achievement. His behavior of making referral calls increased 300 percent within two weeks. He stayed at that level as long as I worked with that agency.

I checked back within a year, and he was still making approximately ten to twelve referral calls every single evening. This may not seem like very much, but for someone who previously had trouble making even one referred-lead call a day, it was a dramatic increase.

This technique can also be used in booking or going on appointments. Another individual I worked with had no trouble making phone calls, but did have great difficulty both qualifying and asking people for appointments. Like me, he enjoyed playing tennis in the evening at his local tennis club in the evening. Left undisciplined, he would usually play tennis from about 2:30 or 3 in the afternoon until 6 or 7 in the evening. He loved tennis so much that we linked it to his behavior of booking appointments.

His goal was to book four appointments per day. As a reward, he would receive time playing tennis in the evening—but only after he booked his four appointments. In this case, by using tennis as a reward, he increased his activity and thereby increased his productivity and profitability 300 to 400 percent within one month.

## Enjoying Production

Giving yourself rewards for an activity you want to increase isn't hard work. It is designed to help you enjoy the underlying activity, whether it be making cold calls or going out on appointments.

Achieving your goal is nice, but since you are linking an activity, such as a cold call, to an enjoyable event such as tennis playing or drinking hot chocolate, you may also begin to more often engage in the activity you may previously have dreaded.

If you link rewards with the activities you want to increase or behaviors you want to change, you will find that there is no limit to the number of changes you can make in yourself—no limit to the modifications you can make to become not only profitable but also happier in your personal life.

## Building Discipline: Eight Weeks to Establishing a Habit Pattern

Rewards not only help increase activity, but can also help instill needed discipline, as well as eliminating feelings of guilt for not hitting your goals.

Individuals around the country frequently ask me about how long it takes to establish a habit pattern. The answer is: between three and eight weeks. If you do anything consistently for three to eight weeks, you can establish a habit pattern.

As we discussed earlier, habits are extremely difficult to break. They are much more easily established. There are good and bad sides to this. It's good because we can ward off nonproductive behaviors or habit patterns that may infect us like viruses—habits like swearing, yelling, tardiness, or anything else you don't want.

But the time it takes to establish a habit has a downside, mainly because it's difficult to do something consistently for three to eight weeks straight without feeling anxious or frustrated. For example, if you decide to start a habit of reading an hour every evening, you may find it very difficult to remember to do it. The frustration comes from having to start over from ground zero to build the habit. We need to do a behavior consistently for this length of time to really make it a habit. The answer is *conditioning theory*: something has to be used to ensure that that habit stays set, like plaster of Paris.

The best example I can give for this is an experiment done by Stanford University in 1982. In this experiment, chimpanzees were taught very simple behaviors that instilled habits. One chimpanzee was given a banana only if he pressed a lever after a light came on two times, followed by a loud buzzer. If he pressed the lever after the first or second light, he would not receive a reward. He would only receive a banana when he pressed the lever after the two lights came on and the buzzer sounded.

As you might have guessed, this habit was established within a three-week period. By three weeks, the chimpanzee would press the lever after the two lights and the buzzer came on, without even receiving the banana as a reward.

The habit was established, but after about three weeks without receiving a reward, the chimpanzee decided that pressing the lever wasn't worth it, so he quit altogether. To get the chimpanzee to hit the lever again, the banana reward was required more frequently. But the researchers decided not to give the chimpanzee a banana after every two lights and a buzzer; instead they gave him one after every tenth or twentieth time the sequence of lights and buzzer occurred. The point is that after the three- to six-week period when your habit is established, consistent daily rewards aren't required anymore. But you do need to maintain your habit by giving yourself an occasional reward, such as a weekend trip, extra television time, or even more time playing tennis. In this way, you can help maintain and solidify that habit.

A good illustration here is a mother whose son swore incessantly. The son had such a foul mouth that the mother felt embarrassed taking him anywhere in public. The ten-year-old was put on a conditioning program in which she tried to develop a habit of not swearing, or rather a habit of keeping a clean mouth. To do this, the mother gave the son $1 every evening, or $7 a week, payable each day without swearing.

After a five-week period, the son did not swear at all. (Note that he was rewarded for keeping a clean mouth and not punished for swearing.) She cut out the $1 daily reward after the five-week period.

The son swore episodically after two months. She then gave the son, randomly, $1 on days that he kept his mouth clean. The reward was random so the son never knew what day he would be rewarded with the $1.

Along with this, the mother didn't buy the son toys or candy. He was required to earn his own money. The son began to feel that the occasional $1 was worth keeping a clean mouth.

## Maintaining Behaviors

Behaviors do need to be maintained, through reinforcement, at least infrequently, and this is really the same idea behind the slot machine. If a slot machine gave you money every time you pulled the "arm" or handle, you would probably keep putting quarters in and pulling the handle until you dropped from exhaustion. But a slot machine is designed to maintain your habit of pulling the handle and putting quarters in by rewarding you, not every time you pull the handle, but infrequently—maybe every tenth, twentieth, or thirtieth time. This is the casino's way of making sure you maintain your established habit of gambling, while they slowly drain you of your cash.

This is the premise on which gambling is based. You become addicted to random rewards. You are rewarded by the casino just enough to keep playing, but not enough to let you win big. At the same time, if you lost money every single time you played, you probably wouldn't gamble. They let you win just enough to keep you playing.

Habits formed and reinforced this way are also the hardest to break. As we discussed earlier, these are called *intermittent rewards*, or *variable-ratio reinforcements*, because you are variably, or randomly, rewarded for activities.

In chapters 16 and 17, you can learn more about how to develop your own conditioning program to change your behaviors and increase your sales production.

# Sixteen
# The Peak Performance Technique

## Incremental Production versus Successive Approximation

After you read this book and apply its concepts, you will probably do a lot more high-priority things on which you previously procrastinated. You will likely become much more productive. You will also make more money, get closer and closer to realizing your goals, and have a lot more fun in your business.

Unfortunately, you'll also find yourself encountering stress as a result of the changes brought about with increased production. Stress results from changes that bring on psychological and physical problems.

### The Psychology of Change

In figure 16.1 (page 189), labeled "Psychology of Change," you will find a graphic model that shows a comfort zone in the middle, bordered on the top by anxiety and on the bottom by depression.

You have probably heard a motivational speaker say, "If you make twenty calls every single day, your business will triple in a year." So you take the speaker up on the advice and make twenty calls. The next day you make fourteen calls, the next day you make ten calls, the fourth day you make five calls, and the fifth day the only call you make is to your mother.

Questions going through of most managers and sales producers are: "Why can't I maintain the high level of activity I want?" Undoubtedly you make more money if you're active. "Why do I have business fluctuations?" "Why am I not making as much money now as I was eighteen months ago? Or even a year ago?"

The answer to these questions lies in your comfort zone. Whatever you are doing in terms of activity right now is in that zone. You feel good at that level, you probably feel comfortable, but, more importantly, it's a level at which you find yourself experiencing no dissonance or distress—at least not enough to change. As soon as you increase your activity, you experience the one thing you probably dread: anxiety. Indications of anxiety are when you begin to feel worried when you are making those twenty phone calls. You feel pressured and pushed. The world is closing in around you; you suddenly have no time; everybody is demanding. Anxiety and distress set in, causing you to drop right back down to the comfort zone, with a lower activity level.

One of the prime reasons New Year's resolutions don't work is that they require too much of a change all at once. A few years ago, I promised myself I would read one book a day. I once was a very fast reader—about 500 to 600 words a minute—but the extra activity, from a half hour to ninety minutes per day, caused anxiety. It wasn't long—about a month—before I dropped right back to my comfort zone of reading only about two or three chapters per night.

FIGURE 16.1 Psychology of Change

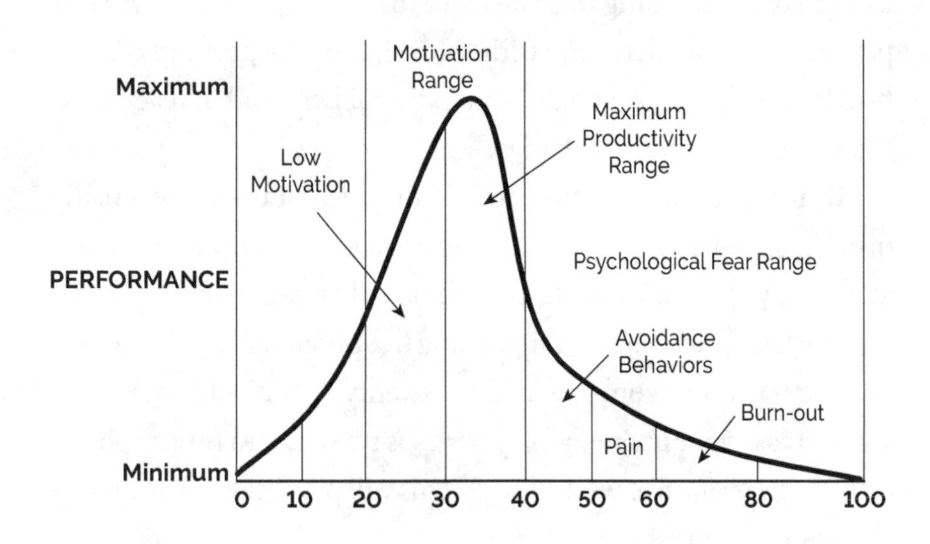


Depression is indicated graphically at the bottom of figure 16.1

What if you did nothing during the day?

What if you just showed up at work?

What if you wasted the day just filing papers or only chatted with coworkers?

If you purchased this book, you are probably a highly motivated person. When you are unproductive, you probably feel guilty. You may be upset for not achieving more. You most likely feel accomplished when you can look back and say, “I got something done today; I did something worthwhile.”

For you, doing nothing promotes depression, lack of motivation, and lethargy, as well as a feeling of worthlessness, low self-esteem, and low self-confidence. Since you don’t like feeling depressed, you jump right back into your comfort zone.

There are actually two ways to achieve your desired change as well as coping with the anxiety created by extra activity. First, make sure you don't increase activity too fast. Do it slowly, so you'll be assured of maintaining that activity. This will help you modify your productivity as well as cope with change. More importantly, it will help keep you from snapping back like a rubber band in reaction to the stress caused by that change.

By using the very simple conditioning techniques we've already discussed, you can really create any change you want and achieve anything you want to do. Just make sure that you do not try to go too quickly, for example, from making five phone calls—which may be in your comfort zone—to making twenty phone calls. Make sure you increase your phone calls by perhaps two a day to twenty phone calls slowly over a five-week period. This will prevent sudden change that results in stress.

## Using SUDS

The second way to manage change is to keep track of your SUDS level (Subjective Unit of Discomfort Scale; see chapter 8, figure 8.1, page 95) and doing the progressive relaxation techniques (see chapter 8) for ninety seconds when your SUDS level is too high. Also take a half hour in total solitude to totally and absolutely relax. This will help you experience less stress on your road to productivity.

## Keep Your Mind on What You Want

When asked why they aren't making more money, many people respond, "I don't want to work that hard." They don't want to experience the stress high activity would bring them. Your activity and effort to achieve a goal by the date that you want will bring change which will also create anxiety and stress. That is, if you don't use the stress-coping techniques I have suggested—including the progressive relaxation technique.

Pace yourself. Don't shoot for the moon within two days and expect to reach it. Work toward it gradually, and you will be assured of gaining anything you could possibly want, and, more important, be happy with it.

Years ago, I watched an interview before the famous George Foreman–Muhammad Ali fight. The interviewer obviously didn't know much about boxing. He asked, "George, you're a guy who's been hit in the face thousands of times, but you still go back for more. How do you do it, George?"

I thought about that, "My gosh! Think of getting hit in the face for a living!"

George Foreman answered, "When I think real hard about what I want, I don't feel the pain. When I think real hard about knocking out my opponent, I don't feel the hits, I don't feel headaches, I don't feel anything. And all I think, taste, hear and see is winning the boxing match."

One of the most profound things that I ever heard came from a man who was a ninth-grade dropout. George Foreman said something that struck me. It all boils down to the idea that when you concentrate on what you want, you don't feel the sacrifice. When you think hard about what you desire, it doesn't seem like such hard work.

In the late 1970s, I got a chance to play some of the greatest tennis pros in the world. When I was on the European Grand Prix Tour, I got a chance to play in Austria, against the national champion from Romania. Besides being a great player, he also was a bit intimidating. In my match I remember feeling a bit nervous, but I was holding my own. Something snapped in the second set of a three-set match.

I was only getting 20 percent of my first serves. In tennis, the first serve is the key. If you can get your first serve in, you can put pressure on your opponent. If you can keep pressure on your opponent, he will make mistakes. Twenty percent first-serve accuracy was not going to win the match. I was gradually losing the set.

In between games, I would walk over to the sideline to grab a drink of water. During one changeover, I remembered a book that came out a few years earlier called *The Inner Game of Tennis*. Written by Tim Galway, it was an extremely innovative work about how a player can change their thought process. I immediately understood I wasn't concentrating on where I wanted the serve to go. I was only focusing on trying to hit the ball with good form and style. That was causing my downfall, because I was concentrating on the details of my service stroke instead of on where I wanted the serve to go.

I took Galway's advice and started concentrating on the exact spot where I wanted to hit the serve, instead of whether my elbow was high or I was reaching up for the ball. As I threw that ball up to serve, all I could think about was the exact spot—a small particle on the court near the Romanian's backhand side, the exact place where I wanted the ball to go after I served. Something magical happened. Every ball I served went to the spot I focused on. When I took my mind off the process of serving—and started concentrating on where I wanted it to go, my first-serve percentage increased to 80 percent.

If you can focus on what you want and not get caught up in the details, if you can think about your goals and not think about the difficulty in achieving them, you'll meet with success you've never experienced before. You also won't feel the deal of pain in the effort. In my experience, most people fear the work that goes into achieving things because of the struggle and stress that goes into it.

## Using Rewards

During the discussion on conditioning techniques, you learned why rewards are really the only means of establishing a behavior or a habit pattern. If, as a child, you got an ice-cream cone for putting your bike away, it wouldn't be long before you put your bike away without having to be reminded. Or perhaps your mother gave you 25 cents every time you helped do the dishes. It wouldn't be long until you did the dishes automatically even without the reward.

To change your habit patterns or increase your productivity, you should give yourself a reward for the things that you want to change.

Look at figure 16.2 (next page), titled "Rewards and Reinforcers." On it are a number of different rewards, ranging from watching TV to going out to dinner. You can even add more rewards at the bottom of the sheet. Make a copy of this sheet so you can include it in the file or notebook you use as your productivity notebook.

To determine what rewards you find most reinforcing, put a check mark next to everything you do that's named in the Rewards and Reinforcers list, whether or not you enjoy doing it. Under the category marked "importance," rate each item you check on a l-to-10 scale (1 is low; 10 is high) according to how enjoyable each of these activities is.

How important is it? How committed are you to doing it? The next category is "time spent." When you do each of these things, how long do you spend doing it or how much do you do it? For example, if you marked down "sports," indicate the number of hours spent playing when you do play, whereas drinking coffee would be expressed in number of cups per day.

Next is frequency.

How often do you do it?

Several times each day?

Once a day?

Once a week?

Mark this down.

The information here that you include in your tailor-made productivity workbook can help you better use your favorite pastimes as rewards to change your habits.

FIGURE 16.2 Rewards and Reinforcers

| ✓ | Activities | Importance | Time Spent | Frequency |
|---|---|---|---|---|
| | Watching television | | | |
| | Listening to the radio | | | |
| | Cup of coffee, Tea | | | |
| | Being alone | | | |
| | Reading a newspaper | | | |
| | Reading a book | | | |
| | Reading a magazine | | | |
| | Exercise (Jogging, Spa, aerobics) | | | |
| | Hobby | | | |
| | Long baths or bubble bath | | | |
| | Eating favorite foods | | | |
| | Going To A Movie, Play, Concert | | | |
| | Sports (tennis, skiing, swimming) | | | |
| | Going out for dinner | | | |
| | | | | |
| | | | | |
| | | | | |

Activity checklist: Check the activities you do, whether or not you enjoy them.

**Importance**: On a 1-to-10 scale, how enjoyable and how important is this activity?

**Time Spent**: When you engage in this activity, how much time do you usually spend?

How much? How many? (For example, two hours, one hour, one cup, one magazine, one apple, etc.)

**Frequency**: How often do you do this activity? (For example, each day, twice per day, once a week, once a month, etc.)

# Seventeen
# The Eight-Week Technique

## Matching Activity Levels and Rewards to the Eight-Week Format

Society has imposed ways to get us to commit to or take responsibility for our actions. It has even found a way to help prevent us from making mistakes. These techniques or mechanisms controls are called *contracts.*

Contracts are such a part of our lives that virtually every man, woman, and child in the United States is under one. In many agreements we enter into, we commit ourselves to keep our word by signing something.

In this chapter, which focuses on behavioral contracts, you will find information on ways to control yourself so that you can accomplish virtually anything you want. You'll also discover ways to reward yourself for activities or behaviors you want to develop in yourself, which in turn will serve to double or even quadruple your income within six to eight weeks. If you successfully complete your simple six- to eight-week behavioral contract, you will find that your productivity, as well as your overall enjoyment and achievement, will skyrocket.

The contract we discuss in this chapter is really a promise or agreement you will make to yourself (you'll ideally also involve another person as your productivity partner) to implement changes on a regular basis to increase your overall performance. The contract is organized so you can change yourself temporarily, as well as permanently, into the person you want to be. It will help you to be financially more profitable and make any amount of money that you are emotionally prepared for.

## Creating Your Own Behavioral Contract

Look at the sample Behavioral Contracts on the next few pages (figures 17.1 through 17.3). On these sheets are a number of categories; on the top are the words "if" and "then."

### THE "IF" COLUMN

The "if" column represents the target behaviors you want to develop. For example, in figure 17.1 (next page), making more referral calls or making more appointments; in figure 17.2 (page 200), gaining a child's cooperation are the target behaviors. Figure 17.3 (page 201) is a blank sheet you can use as a model for your own behavioral contract. Make a copy of your behavioral contract and include it in your productivity file or notebook.

Fill this "if" section in with statements such as "If I make six cold calls each day . . ." or "If I book one appointment per day . . ." or "If Johnny puts his toys away . . ."

Record each step you have planned.

FIGURE 17.1 **Sample Behavioral Contract for Oneself**

**EFFECTIVE DATES:** From ________________ To ________________

**IF** I make three contacts each day and If I book one appointment each day,

**THEN** I will receive one cup of coffee after I book the appointment and can read my favorite book.

**IF** I go on one appointment each day,

**THEN** I can play tennis in the evening or see a friend on the way home.

**IF** I achieve my goal each and every day for the week for contacts, booked appointments, and face-to-face appointments,

**THEN** My wife and I can go out to dinner at the restaurant of my choice.

**BONUS:** ________________

**CONTROL:** My wife will meet with me every day to discuss my goal activity and help me keep track. I will give $100 to my wife for security. If I give myself a reward without earning it, or fall off the program before eight weeks are completed, she may spend the $100 as she pleases.

________________ ________________
(signed) Goal Achiever (date)

________________ ________________
(signed) Partner (date)

This contract will be reviewed on ________________ (date)

FIGURE 17.2 **Behavioral Contract for Child's Behavior**

**EFFECTIVE DATES: From** ______________ **To** ______________

**IF** Johnny succeeds in picking up each day and being well-behaved all week and earns his rewards each day,

**THEN** I will take him to the play area of his choice (park, beach, etc.) for one hour or more on the weekend.

**IF** Johnny picks up his room,

**THEN** I will give him one toy army man immediately and praise him.

**IF** Johnny picks up any of his toys, clothes, etc. in his room,

**THEN** I will give him 50 cents just before he goes to bed and praise him during the day.

**BONUS:** ______________

**CONTROL:** I will deposit $100 with my spouse, which will be refunded if I complete the eight-week program with Johnny and if I give Johnny the rewards when he has earned them. I promise to meet with my spouse daily to review Johnny's target behavior activity and his attitude. If the program is not completed within eight weeks, she may spend the $100 as she pleases.

______________ **(signed) Goal Achiever** ______________ **(date)**

______________ **(signed) Partner** ______________ **(date)**

**This contract will be reviewed on** ______________ **(date)**

FIGURE 17.3 Blank Behavioral Contract

**EFFECTIVE DATES: From** ____________ **To** ____________

**IF** ____________ **THEN** ____________

**IF** ____________ **THEN** ____________

**IF** ____________ **THEN** ____________

**BONUS:** ____________

**CONTROL:** ____________

____________ ____________
(signed) Goal Achiever (date)

____________ ____________
(signed) Partner (date)

This contract will be reviewed on ____________ (date)

## THE "THEN" COLUMN

The "then" statements denote the reward you will give yourself for changing your behavior, or, in some cases, the reward someone else will give you. The "then" becomes a consequence only of fulfilling the "if" statement.

Below an "if" statement such as "If I make five phone calls each day," you might write,

"Then I can watch the evening news."

"If Johnny puts his toys away each evening . . . ,"

"Then I will give him 25 cents."

The "then" part of the contract can be drawn from your Rewards and Reinforcers sheet (figure 16.2). Any reward can be used if you've rated it an enjoyment level of at least 6. It's something you should give yourself if you earn it—but not before you earn it.

Rewards do and will work to increase your performance, but only if you use them as directed in the program. Link the reward directly to the target behavior—don't defer your reward any more than a few hours. For example, you wouldn't link the reward of golf to a daily increase in referral calls, since you probably can't golf every day. However, golf could be a weekly bonus.

## THE "BONUS" COLUMN

Directly beneath the "if" and "then" columns is a line labeled "bonus." The bonus is a reward for successfully accomplishing the weekly goals and activities you set for yourself. This bonus can be something like a dinner at a nice restaurant on Saturday night after completing a week's goals. Anything you think would be rewarding would help reinforce your motivation to accomplish goals during the week, thereby increasing your productivity.

### YOUR PRODUCTIVITY PARTNER

Directly below the bonus section, write in the name of your productivity partner. Choose somebody—ideally a spouse or someone you work with and trust—who can help you enforce this contract and encourage you throughout the six- to eight-week program you are embarking upon. This individual should be someone you see daily, someone who can discuss your goals and accomplishments with you, and someone who can commit to supporting your efforts for at least six to eight weeks.

Since we often rationalize ourselves into giving ourselves a reward even when we haven't earned it, a partner is not only a good idea but is truly necessary to help keep you on track.

To help keep you committed to this program, write a check to your partner for $100 or more. If you fall short of your contractual obligations, or if you fail to give yourself a designated reward, or if you decide before the six- to eight-week termination point that you want to quit this program for any reason except changing your goals, you forfeit the $100 to your partner. If you quit before the eight-week period is up, you should tell your partner to cash the check and spend it any way he or she sees fit.

While this is a difficult commitment, if you sincerely want to commit yourself to achieving your goal by your target date, it is a small price to pay.

## Defining Your Goals

Now select the goal you wish to start working toward during the next eight weeks. If it is a major goal, like making $100,000 a year, break it down into segments so you know exactly how much work you need to do to make steady progress every month, every week, and, if you can determine it, every day. If your goal is making $100,000, divide it by twelve. This will tell you the amount you need to make each month—around $8,500. If you break it down further, you need to make about $2,000 a week, and you can even break that down to a daily target if you like.

## Contracting to Get Your Goals

A computer-accessories salesman whom I worked with for eight weeks had this goal: he wanted a 31-foot Pearson yacht. It cost approximately $50,000. The salesman earned only about $2,000 a month. He sold around two products a week—eight products a month—and his average commission was approximately $250, so you can see that it would be difficult, at best, for him to buy a yacht or even lease it.

He also set a goal for himself to purchase that yacht within two months. Since his goal depended on generating a larger income, he needed to increase the number of products he sold. His averages dictated that to get one sale, he must see about two prospects. To hit that goal, he needed to book about three appointments. To book three appointments, he needed to call ten referred leads. His average activity showed that he was calling approximately twenty referrals a week. He was booking about six appointments a week and seeing about two prospects a week, which yielded him two sales per week, for a weekly grand total of $500.

The lease on the yacht would cost him around $600 a month. That meant generating about three more sales per month. This translated into calling thirty more referrals per month, or almost eight more referrals a week. He would also have to book nine more appointments and see six more prospects per month. This would have to be done over and beyond the number of sales he needed to maintain his standard of living.

So to start leasing the yacht on the date he wanted, he would only have to work a little harder to increase his activity. If this seems to you like a lot more work, keep in mind the law of forced efficiency, which holds that if you push yourself to do something, you'll always find an easier way to do it. In this particular example, this salesperson, when faced with making more calls, found easier ways to make referral calls and tended to qualify the people he was prospecting much more effectively. Eventually he wasn't doing that much more activity; he was just improving his efficiency and, as a result, his productivity. He wasn't working more; he was just working smarter.

The way we started my client on the program was very simple. We knew he was currently making around four referral calls per day, booking about one appointment per day, and seeing around one prospect per day. He was also making one sale, on the average, every two days. Although he ultimately would have to increase his activity, we started him at his current normal activity level, to try to get him used to the program. His Rewards and Reinforcers sheet indicated he enjoyed, on an importance level of 6 or more, watching television, playing tennis, and drinking coffee. He also enjoyed going out to dinner on the weekends.

Coffee drinking was linked to calls. For every call he made, he could take a sip or drink of his coffee. If he made no phone calls, he received no coffee that day. Since he also liked to watch television in the evening, we linked television time—about an hour—to appointments, so if he went on an appointment, he could watch one hour of television. No appointments that day, no television.

The last reward we linked to an activity was tennis. Since my client really enjoyed playing tennis a couple of times a week, we linked seeing prospects to tennis. For every two prospects he saw (usually he saw two a day), he would receive an afternoon or evening of playing tennis.

There was no reward given for the number of sales he made. If his activity increased, we knew sales would follow. No salesperson will be active or increase activity for very long without having sales go up a proportional amount.

The bonus for this salesman was that if he accomplished his goals for the week, namely making four referral calls per day, booking one appointment per day, and seeing one prospect per day, he could go out to a nice restaurant and have a wonderful dinner as a reward.

During the second week, my client increased his phone calls by one per day. It wasn't until the fourth week that he also increased his booked appointments, as well as the number of prospects he saw during the day.

By making a slow, steady increase, he was able to adjust to the extra activity, preventing stress and strain. He also adjusted to rewarding himself or not giving himself rewards, depending on the activity he performed.

By the eighth week, he had approximately tripled the number of sales he was making because he had tripled the amount of activity he was doing before sales. It didn't take him long to triple his sales without working any harder. He just learned to work smarter and better.

In another case, I worked with a manager who didn't make phone calls but found he either did not have or take the time to read more business-related articles and books. His target behavior was to spend more time reading, thereby building his management skills. His goal was to read two extra books per month. Breaking that down, he needed to read ten more pages, or one chapter, per day. The benefit or improving his management skills would be that he would be more valuable to his company and make more money.

Gaining improved skills from his reading also made his job more interesting. We started this manager off by getting him to read one more page per day. It usually took him only about one to two minutes. But just getting the book out, looking at the page, and reading it was enough to start the habit pattern. In time we would increase that. But at first it was more important just to gett a book in front of him.

We found from his Rewards and Reinforcers sheet that he enjoyed walking around the block at noon. Walking, on his scale of importance, was an 8. Every time he read one page, he could have his noon walk. After the third and fourth week, he was awarded with a walk for every five pages. By increasing slowly, he was reading ten pages or one chapter per day after six weeks. If he met his reading goals each of the five workdays, his bonus was earning eighteen holes of golf.

A final example of behavioral contracts involves the case of a real-estate salesperson. This realtor's goal was to be able to buy a house by the end of a twelve-month period. The house had a $1,000 monthly mortgage. To hit this goal, she needed to sell one more house every month, giving her an extra $1,000 commission. Since only one out of every two escrows closed, she really needed to sell two extra houses per month to close one extra escrow per month. Her averages showed that to close one sale, she needed to show eight houses. To show eight houses, she needed to book sixteen appointments, because of high fallout. To book sixteen appointments, she needed to make 160 phone calls per month.

Spread over a week, this proved very simple. Since she needed to sell one more house per month, she needed to go on two more showings per week, to book four more appointments per week, and to make around forty more referral calls per week. This came out to eight calls per day, one booked appointment per day, and one showing every two days. Broken down daily, this seemed to be less work than anticipated. In other words, she really needed to double her activity so she could afford to buy the house within one year.

Again, I started her off at current activity levels, not wanting to increase too quickly for fear too much change would create anxiety.

Her Rewards and Reinforcers sheet indicated she smoked cigarettes, rating it a 7. While this is not a good idea in the long term, she wasn't likely to quit anytime soon, so we used it to create a habit in another area. She also enjoyed seeing friends in the evening, which she rated a 7. She also enjoyed jogging, rating that an 8.

She could smoke one cigarette after she made one referral call. She smoked ten cigarettes per day, so after the eighth call—her goal for the day—she could smoke as many as she wanted.

Since she also enjoyed jogging, she was rewarded with jogging in the evening if and only if she booked one appointment to show a house that day. Since she enjoyed seeing friends, every time she showed a house, she would reward herself with a visit. Since she only showed a house every two days, this rewarded her with frequent visits to friends—but only if she first showed a property.

As in other cases, we didn't increase her activity very quickly. It was done on a slow and methodical basis, so after around eight weeks, her activity had reached the point where she was selling one extra house per month and putting herself well on track to reaching her twelve-month goal of buying a new house with a $1,000 monthly mortgage.

## Know Your Averages

Now take the time to write down your own averages. If you're unsure how to do this, please refer to chapters 11 and 12 on averages, or to figures 17.4 and 17.5.

Please write down your current weekly and daily activity in a log, and compare this to your target behavior (see figures 17.6 through 17.9).

FIGURE 17.4 What Are Your Averages?

1 sale = # appointments = # booked appointments = # calls

OR

1 sale = what target activity?

(For example: 1 sale = 3 appointments = 4 booked appointments = 40 calls)

If 1 sale = $800 commission, then 1 call = $20

Finally, break down your goal and decide how much more activity you will need to achieve your objective by the date you have specified. Next, start linking the rewards or reinforcers to each target behavior. You should now have a good idea of how fast and when to increase your activity—for example, the number of calls and appointments—so you can reach the target behavior and deadline you've set.

**FIGURE 17.5** Current Activity

**What are you currently doing each day and week to reach your goal?**

Number of sales per week or day?

Number of appointments per week or day?

Number of booked appointments per week or day?

Number of calls per week or day?

**Other Target Behaviors**

Tardiness: How often are you late (or on time)?

Reading: How many pages are you currently reading each day/week?

How often does your child misbehave?

How often does your child follow instructions?

How many pounds do you want to lose?

**FIGURE 17.6** Weekly Activity Sheet: Sales

| Client | Appointment Booked | Appointment Kept | Contacts |
|---|---|---|---|
| SUNDAY | | | |
| | | | |
| | | | |
| | | | |
| | | | |
| | | | |
| MONDAY | | | |
| Don Morris 237-1120 | X | | XXXXX |
| Tim Donaldson 426-1181 | X | | |
| Donna Blake 847-2222 | X | | |
| | | | |
| | | | |

| Client | Appointment Booked | Appointment Kept | Contacts |
|---|---|---|---|
| TUESDAY | | | |
| Fred James 827-1052 | X | | XXXXX<br>XX |
| Tom Jana 811-1361 | X | | |
| Tim Parker 832-2136 | | X | |
| Steve Jamison 831-2922 | | X | |
| | | | |
| WEDNESDAY | | | |
| Jim Jones 840-2722 | X | | XXXXX<br>XXXXX<br>XX |
| Tom Linwood 832-0100 | X | | |
| Dick Lester 640-1237 | X | | |
| Donna Blake 847-222 | | X | |
| Tim Donaldson 426-1181 | | X | |
| THURSDAY | | | |
| Fred Perkins 640-1962 | X | | XXXXX<br>XXXXX<br>XXX |
| John Fredricks 840-1962 | X | | |
| Janet Edwards 638-4026 | X | | |
| Fred James 827-1052 | | X | |
| Tom Jana 811-1361 | | X | |
| FRIDAY | | | |
| Fritz Perry 744-7377 | X | | XXXXX<br>XXXXX |
| Tom Montgomery 882-6449 | X | | |
| Frank Thompson 540-6266 | X | | |
| Tom Linwood 837-1011 | | X | |
| | | | |
| SATURDAY | | | |
| | | | |
| | | | |
| | | | |
| | | | |
| | | | |

Each time you make a call, put an X under "Contacts."

Each time you book an appointment, put an X under "Appointment Booked" with name, phone number, time, and date booked.

Each time you actually go on an appointment, put an X under "Appointment Kept" with name, phone number, and time and date completed.

FIGURE 17.7 **Weekly Child's Behavior Sheet**

| Child's target behavior: Pick up toys | Number of times | Goal Achieved | Reward given |
|---|---|---|---|
| SUNDAY | | | |
| | | | |
| | | | |
| MONDAY | | | |
| Picked up blanket | X | yes | yes |
| TUESDAY | | | |
| Picked up books, papers, blankets | XXX | yes | yes |
| WEDNESDAY | | | |
| Without my asking, John picked up books, blankets and clothes | XXXX | yes | yes |
| THURSDAY | | | |
| Didn't pick up anything even when asked | | no | no |
| FRIDAY | | | |
| Without my asking, again he picked up all toys, clothes; room very neat | XXX | yes | yes |
| SATURDAY | | | |
| Picked up everything | XXXXXX | yes | yes |

FIGURE 17.8 Weekly Activity Sheet: Reading

| Title of Book | Goal: pages read | Pages read | Reward given |
|---|---|---|---|
| SUNDAY | | | |
| See You At The Top | 2 | 2 | yes |
| | | | |
| MONDAY | | | |
| See You At The Top | 3 | 3 | yes |
| Spike | 5 | 5 | |
| TUESDAY | | | |
| See You At The Top | 6 | 0 | no |
| Spike | 6 | 6 | |
| WEDNESDAY | | | |
| See You At The Top | 7 | 7 | yes |
| Spike | 7 | 7 | |
| THURSDAY | | | |
| See You At The Top | 10 | 10 | yes |
| Spike | 10 | 10 | |
| FRIDAY | | | |
| See You At The Top | 14 | 14 | yes |
| Spike | 14 | 14 | |
| SATURDAY | | | |
| | | | |
| | | | |

**FIGURE 17.9** Weekly Activity Sheet

| Activities | | | |
|---|---|---|---|
| SUNDAY | | | |
| | | | |
| | | | |
| | | | |
| MONDAY | | | |
| | | | |
| | | | |
| | | | |
| TUESDAY | | | |
| | | | |
| | | | |
| | | | |
| WEDNESDAY | | | |
| | | | |
| | | | |
| | | | |
| THURSDAY | | | |
| | | | |
| | | | |
| | | | |
| FRIDAY | | | |
| | | | |
| | | | |
| | | | |
| SATURDAY | | | |
| | | | |
| | | | |
| | | | |

Clients sometimes say, "Kerry, I'm only making two phone calls a day now, and I'm going on about one appointment a day, but my objective is to make twenty phone calls. I'll just do that tomorrow." This is exactly what happens at New Year's resolution time, when you promise that you'll stop smoking starting on January 2. Then all of a sudden you realize it's August, and you're moking more than ever. Some people make New Year's promises to themselves to make more phone calls or go on more appointments, yet nothing ever changes.

The real reason for this is that you may expect too much of yourself too quickly, and you may think you can instantly change habit patterns by willpower only. This rarely works.

The truth is that you need to have a systematic program by which you can change gradually; without such a program, you may never see improvement or change.

I encourage you to increase your activity after the first week of using reinforcers or as soon as you feel comfortable with the program. The idea, however, is to start at your present levels of activity. Ask yourself, "What level am I achieving right now?" Start at that level for about a week or two until you get used to the program and to maintaining the same amount of activity, and then increase your activity.

For example, I worked with a car salesperson who was very excited about reaching her goals within one year. She started out on this program at her present activity levels—meeting with about three people and making five referral phone calls per day. In turn, she was giving herself one piece of candy for every referral call she made, and around one half hour of television for every appointment she went on. She kept herself at this five-call-three-appointment phase for about two weeks, even though it was not a change from her normal activity. She gave herself a chance to adapt to accepting rewards and being on the program. Over the next two to three weeks, as she felt more comfortable with the rewards and the program, she started increasing her activity to six phone calls and four appointments per day; then seven phone calls; and then eight phone calls and five appointments a day.

Don't push yourself too hard too fast at the beginning of this program. Make sure you are totally comfortable with giving yourself rewards. Just as importantly, make sure to give yourself a reward when you have earned it. One of the most important concepts of this program is that when you've earned a reward, you *must* take it. If you don't give yourself a reward when you've earned it, the likelihood you'll achieve your objectives by the date that you want is very low.

## Successive Approximation

The concept behind increasing activity slowly is called *successive approximation*. We use successive approximation to learn to do things or to overcome fears. For example, if you have a fear of elevators, a psychologist wouldn't take you up to the top floor and say, "Look at what I did for you—you're cured," while you're on the elevator floor screaming, crying, and pounding the walls. They would start by taking you up to the steps that lead to the elevator, and then back. On the second day, you'd both go up to the elevator door, then stop and go home. By the third day, you'd both go inside the elevator, but not up or down in it. On the fourth day, you'd both go only one floor, and then continue until you became comfortable with the elevator. Every time your anxiety increased—along with your SUDS level (see chapter 8) went up, too—in response to being close to or on the elevator, the psychologist would help you relax. He or she would ask you to take three or four deep breaths as you gradually eliminated your elevator phobia.

With this program, working a little at a time towards your goal will be much more effective than trying to do too much too fast.

## Your Bonus—That Certain Something Extra

Now look at the bonus column on the behavioral contracts in figures 17.1 through 17.3. This bonus column is really meant to give you something extra—an extra reward for accomplishing what you set out to do that week. For example, if your objective was to make five referral phone calls per day and one appointment per day, and if you did make twenty-five calls and five appointments that week, then you could give yourself a nice bonus on the weekend. Perhaps you might go out to dinner with your spouse or take the whole day off and just going golfing. Obviously, if you didn't accomplish your goals, you couldn't take the dinner or go golfing.

You cannot take the bonus if you don't earn it. But it's critical to take the bonus when you do earn it. Make sure it's something you really want. If going out to dinner is something that only your spouse wants to do, and you're just going along with the idea, it won't work. After all, this is *your* program.

## Your Police Officer

As I pointed out earlier in the chapter, it's also a good idea to give your performance partner a check for $100, $200, or even $300—whatever would hurt the most without being financially burdensome.

This is only a deposit, which will be refunded to you only after you successfully complete the program. This deposit will also help ensure that you take the reward when you deserve it.

Never give yourself a reward if you don't deserve it. Stay on the program for at least six to eight weeks until you do dramatically increase your productivity and activity. If you stick out the eight weeks, you will change and your goals will come true.

As a control, you should promise to interact with your partner—whether an office mate or your spouse—about your progress on the program at least once a day; you should also promise to complete a daily and weekly activity sheet, like the ones shown in figures 17.6 through 17.9. Figure 17.9 is a blank weekly activity sheet for you to use as a model and include in the file or notebook you use as your sales-performance workbook. The weekly activity sheet will enable your partner to see how you have been doing.

Your partner is really your police officer. This is the person you've designated to monitor and be supportive of your efforts to reach the goals. By filling out a "Weekly/Daily Activity Sheet," you're keeping a log of what you do each day and each week, as well as giving your partner a chance to see what your activity has been. You can also use the sheet to decide whether or not you've earned a reward.

## Remember to Reward Yourself

I can't stress enough how important it is to take a reward when you've earned one. It is important to watch television if you earned it by making phone calls or by reading a certain number of pages you've scheduled for yourself that day. More important, however, is making sure you get *immediate* rewards. A deferred reward is something like getting paid a salary every two weeks, while an immediate reward is getting something immediately, such as praise. Immediate rewards help you increase your activity much faster.

Many people I've worked with have given themselves a glass of fruit juice for every phone call they make. Or they give themselves a candy bar, or maybe a couple of nuts.

During toilet training, every parent in America should know that praise is important. But one thing that works even better than praise is giving the child a reward like M&Ms. Amazingly, when children receive rewards like this they can't wait to get back to the toilet. You can cut in half the time it takes to toilet-train a child. It usually takes anywhere from three to ten weeks. But parents who give immediate reward like M&Ms often toilet-train in two weeks or sometimes less.

Give yourself an immediate reward after you do your target behavior. Whether it's eating a piece of candy, drinking a sip of juice, or taking a break to talk to a friend, I encourage you to take these immediate rewards every time you do the target behavior.

## Using Tokens

Another way to use an immediate reward to increase your activity or increase your target behavior is using tokens. Often you can't eat a piece of candy after every phone call. Sometimes you make twenty calls, and you'd probably make yourself sick eating candy each time. Or maybe sometimes you may not feel like drinking orange juice or taking a bite of an apple.

Tokens work equally well to give you an immediate reward at times when you don't want your usual reward. Tokens are one of the best ways to reinforce behavior, because you can give yourself one token even when you're not hungry or thirsty for your reward.

Tokens can be used anytime, anywhere. They can be such things as poker chips, pennies, or even paper clips. Tokens are rewards you can use in two ways:

1. Write on your behavioral contract that you will receive one token for every phone call that you make. Each token might represent one half-hour of television time or a cup of coffee. For every five tokens, you might receive tennis time, or an hour of playing golf at the range in the evening. For every ten tokens, for example, you might receive time doing pleasure reading that evening.

2. You can also use tokens by themselves to change your behavior. If you are working on being more assertive with your prospects or clients, then you would give yourself a paper clip or a poker chip whenever you feel you have been assertive. This serves to help increase your self-esteem and make you feel proud that you really are improving your behavior. Giving yourself a token also helps you keep in mind your goal of becoming more assertive. As a result, using tokens can really help increase your self-esteem as you accumulate more and more of them.

You might decide to use tokens as a means of helping you get more referrals. At first you could give yourself a token for even thinking about asking a client for a referral. Later on in the week or month, you could give yourself a token only if you actually asked a client for five referrals. And then, later on, you could give yourself a token only if a client actually gave you referrals.

I worked with a securities broker who worked in the California branch of a prestigious New York–based stock brokerage firm. He had the perpetual problem of being late in the morning. Because of the three-hour time difference, the NYSE opens at 7 a.m. Los Angeles time. My client was not a morning person—he was more of a night owl. He came alive in the late afternoon. But he wanted to get to the office earlier. His tardiness was really an avoidance behavior, a fear symptom.

To get himself to the office on time, he would give himself a token. I put one slight modification in his behavioral contract. Every time he got to the office early—whether it was only five or ten minutes—he would give himself two tokens. Interestingly, he found himself wanting to get to work early, not because it was important to his boss, but because he wanted to get that token.

A friend of mine is a psychologist who worked with the University of Michigan football team. The University of Michigan Wolverines are perennially among the best NCAA college football teams in the country. They're ferocious. Those young men will do anything for their team.

But that team was not always as successful. Years ago the Wolverines' psychologist decided that tokens might be an effective tool for getting the players to tackle harder, fumble less, and recover fumbles more frequently. On the advice of the psychologist, the coaching staff started putting little stickers on the players' helmets for every big tackle they made or for every fumble they recovered. The ends and the wide receivers received stickers for every catch they made. The coaching staff found that these players would do almost anything to get one of the stickers. They would jump over defenders, mow people down, and practically go through brick walls.

If you're on an opposing football team lined up across the scrimmage line from a football player who has a helmet full of stickers, it's a little intimidating. You know that player must have done something right to get all those tokens.

It's a lot like the Army's way of giving stripes to denote rank or valor. For every heroic act, or any other achievement, he or she gets a little emblem on the uniform. This is an interesting way of receiving tokens. Recognition through a reward that all can see and admire is often more valued than money, which is itself just another token.

Here's another example of how effective tokens can be. I recently talked to a mother who was having a problem with her son's behavior. He would race out of his room in the morning, not picking up any toys, not making his bed, not putting his clothes away.

The mother tried spanking. She tried yelling at the child. But nothing seemed to work for long. Obviously the child would try to avoid punishment by picking up his toys, but that would usually last only about two or three days—certainly not more than a week. I told her frankly that the child needed a much more physical form of reward than just praise and certainly something different from punishment. Since her son liked to play army, I told her to give the child army men as a token reward. She responded, "What if he doesn't do anything that I can reward him for?"

This is a popular misconception. Every child does something—however small—that somewhat approximates a behavior you want it to do. For example, this child at least looked at his clothes before he left them and left the room in a shambles. He at least threw all of his toys on top of the bed before he left his room in the morning. I told the mother to reward the child for any behavior that was even close to what she wanted.

She first started rewarding the child with one toy army man just for picking up one toy from the floor. Next she rewarded him with a man only for putting the toys away. She then rewarded the child only for throwing clothes into one corner of the room, instead of all over the room. Next she rewarded him with an army man only for putting dirty clothes in the hamper, and then, finally, for hanging up clothes in his closet. She was steadily rewarding the child first for things that were close to what she wanted, and ultimately, after two or three weeks, only for exactly what she wanted. She was surprised not only at how fast this program worked, but also at how long the child continued to pick up his clothes. He didn't go back to his old habits, as he did when she just screamed at him or punished him with a spanking. She randomly rewarded the child with an army man to maintain the habit pattern.

In another case, I worked with a client who wanted to lose weight. One of the toughest things we can do is lose weight once we have set a habit of overeating. This guy was around fifty pounds overweight. He told me he exercised (which I doubted). More importantly, he told me he was on a diet that wasn't working. Diets usually do work over a long period of time, but most people will stay on a diet for only about two days and then go back to eating their lemon-meringue pie. My client carried poker chips in one of his suit pockets. At first, he rewarded himself a token of a poker chip every time he thought about resisting a high-calorie food. The following week, his only reward was for eating a salad, or food he knew was consistent with his diet. Finally, towards the end of the program, he was only rewarded for a whole day of staying on his diet, plus exercise. He gave himself an extra token for that.

After the fourth or fifth week, not only would he have a low-calorie drink for breakfast, a salad for lunch, and a low-calorie meal for dinner, he would also have to run one mile during the day. Only if he accomplished those things would he get a token. He did indeed develop a habit of staying on his diet, plus exercising. He lost weight faster using this method than anything else he had tried.

You can also use tokens in your business life. Give yourself a token after every phone call you make or every appointment you book. If you aren't yet at that stage, give yourself a token every time you even think about making a phone call or booking an appointment.

With your tailor-made Peak Performance Program, you'll be surprised how quickly you can change behaviors to do exactly what you should. By sticking to your behavioral contract—giving yourself rewards and tokens when you deserve them and not giving yourself them when you don't deserve them—you'll find that your business will increase dramatically and you will carry out your target behaviors faster than you ever thought possible. Follow your contract as closely as possible. If you have any questions or comments, please call me at my office 714-730-3560.

I would love to hear from you. Please also write me:

Dr. Kerry Johnson
P.O. Box 1404
Tustin, California 92681.
Kerry@KerryJohnson.com
Linked In: Kerry Johnson, MBA, PhD
Twitter: #DrKerryJohnson

Stay on this program for eight weeks. Remember to use conditioning techniques to help instead of hurt you, and remember how you can rid yourself of your self-sabotaging fears. If you apply these techniques, your productivity will skyrocket to heights you never before thought possible.

Use this Peak Performance System. Follow the techniques outlined. You'll be very glad you did.

CPSIA information can be obtained
at www.ICGtesting.com
Printed in the USA
LVHW030227130819
627393LV00006B/7/P